Wholehearted Purpose

WOMEN DISCOVERING THEIR ONE-OF-A-KIND DESIGN

Mary Tomlinson

Write Way Publishing Company

Printed in the United States of America
ISBN 978-0-9976076-6-6

Write Way
Publishing Company
Print . Digital . Audio
Write Way Publishing
Company LLC

DEDICATION

To the one who is
God's greatest blessing to me
and the love of my life,
Bill Tomlinson,
and our two amazing and super-fun
adult children, Sarah and David—
each living beautiful expressions
of their individual God-ordained
On-Purpose lives.

Wholehearted Purpose

ENDORSEMENTS

"Mary Tomlinson is the quintessential leader with a heart for people in the now and an incredible vision for leaders of tomorrow. Without hesitation I believe Mary Tomlinson is one of the best communicators in helping people to discover their purpose. Her ability to connect with people is God-given, and I am personally inspired, encouraged, and challenged each and every time I listen to her."

Michael Chatman, President & CEO
The Center of Generosity at Cape Coral Foundation
Host, The Giving Show

"Mary Tomlinson is an inspiration to me in countless ways. Through her wise counsel, I clarified my unique purpose and discovered how it plays out in every facet of my family, work, leadership, ministry, and community life. That clarity renewed my focus and energy toward God's plan for my life. *Wholehearted Purpose* is a treasure."

Lisa Schultz, Chief Services Officer
CNL Financial Group

"You are not an accident! God created you for a purpose. Knowing that purpose opens the door to live and give in God's image—the greatest Giver of all. Mary's work has helped women in every season of life move from unsure of their impact to joyfully on-purpose for the Kingdom. Give yourself a gift and read *Wholehearted Purpose*. You'll be deeply encouraged and discover a new and vibrant way to live."

Pamela Pugh, Chairman of the Board
Women Doing Well Initiatives

"When women identify and embrace their unique, God-given passion and calling, there's no stopping them! Women living 'on-purpose' will powerfully impact their home, workplace, community, and beyond. Mary Tomlinson will show you how to live each day joyfully to the glory of God and for the advancement of His Kingdom. Explore your one-of-a-kind purpose through this inspiring book . . . and discover what you might be missing!"

Leslie Bennett
Women's Ministry Initiatives
Revive Our Hearts Ministry

"A delightful and engaging read about women who through the 'On-Purpose Process' are able to succinctly articulate their reason for being, giving clarity and focus surrounding use of their God-given time and talents. Thought-provoking questions encourage you to do the same. A joy!"

Cynthia Koerner
Chief Financial Officer
Young Life

"Coach, speaker, author, and business advisor, Mary Tomlinson submits a straight-forward guide and practical advice on living a life 'on purpose.' Mary weaves her own personal stories and over 30 years of experience, to encourage women to know who they are and point them to the importance of having a relationship with Christ. This book will serve as an excellent guide to any woman desiring to make her life count."

Monica Rose Brennan, Associate Professor and
Director of Women's Ministries, Liberty University
Author, *Marvelously Made*

"Have you lost your way because you have lost your why? You must read *Wholehearted Purpose* by my fabulous friend Mary, whose heart is most alive when she is helping others find their God-given purpose. *Wholehearted Purpose* is inspiring, helpful, and life changing. Here is a road map to discover your purpose and the tools to help you find your why!"

Jody Jean Dreyer, Former Disney Executive
Advisor; speaker; author, *Unpacking the Castle*

"The beauty of this book is that it guides readers to find their passion and also helps them live it out. The stories are both inspirational to read and provide insightful 'how tos.' Mary shares her wisdom in an approachable and engaging manner. Bravo!"

Susan Braun, Chief Executive Officer
The V Foundation for Cancer Research

"This book is quintessential Mary. It captures not only her purposeful communication style but also draws out the passion and purpose in others. It's a must-read for anyone who wants to live the life they were designed to live."

Robert C. Rauf, Jr., CLU, ChFC
Wealth Management Advisor, Meridian Financial

"As a journalist, I am a fan of stories that inspire, point to truth, and enlighten—and this book is chock full of them! I was deeply touched by the vulnerability and authenticity with which these women share their journeys to an on-purpose life. These rich stories inspired me to go more deeply into discovering my own purpose. Mary always leaves me feeling encouraged, uplifted, and pointed to the life Christ ordained for me."

Amanda Ober, News Reporter
WESH-TV, Orlando, Florida

"Nothing is more powerful than your personal parable—your unique story on how God has perfectly wired you to fulfill His purpose in your life. Through her compilation of dozens of heart-touching, painfully transparent, and compelling journeys, Mary Tomlinson has plowed a critically important field for women (and men) on how to definitively discover your purpose. Read, digest, and then implement the simple, powerful, and time-tested path powerfully unveiled by Mary Tomlinson in *Wholehearted Purpose*."

Dr. Jim Harris
Award-winning author of 14 books including *Our Unfair Advantage: How to Unleash the Power of the Holy Spirit in Your Business*

"There are many books on discovering purpose, but *Wholehearted Purpose* is unique. Mary Tomlinson shares a collection of stories from real women who discovered their purpose using the tools in this book. Each woman experienced her own personal 'aha' moment, and Mary generously shares how anyone can discover their purpose."

Kim King, author
***When Women Give* (August 2017)**

Acknowledgments

First, I want to thank my business partner, Kevin W. McCarthy, the author of *The On-Purpose Person*, *The On-Purpose Business Person*, and *On-Purpose Peace*. He has been a tireless pioneer for the message of purpose, and I am deeply grateful for his profound and transformational insights on the On-Purpose Person Process.

Since 2002 when we began working together, his heart always has been to generously share the message so that more individuals and organizations can understand their unique, God-given purpose. He has deeply impacted me and my lifework and has always been a wonderful On-Purpose cheerleader, friend, and mentor.

I want to thank every amazing woman whom I have had the privilege to coach through the On-Purpose Person Process. Thank you for your trust and giving me the distinct honor of walking beside you in what is a sacred endeavor to understand who God made you to be and become. It has blessed my socks off to see God at work in your lives!

Thank you to the Women Doing Well team and the thousands of women who have attended the Igniting Generous Joy conferences. These women encouraged me to write this book about Wholehearted Purpose and they read, edited, suggested changes, and loved me throughout. In each of our lives, we need those who will push us farther than we ever thought we could go—and this group has encouraged me to step out in faith to see what God might do.

They say "it takes a village"—and I am indebted to those who came alongside me in the development of all aspects of the book you hold in your hands. Thank you to Julie Holzmann, Julie Wilson, Janice Worth, Marissa O'Brien, Angie and Carson Cheatham, Rachel Poel, James Kinnard, Lee Heinrich, and Charlotte Sinclaire.

My deepest debt of gratitude is to my husband of thirty-eight years, Bill Tomlinson—the one who has always steadfastly believed in me during my many times of doubt. Without you, I would never have discovered my own purpose or passion for this work. Thank you for always gently and lovingly pushing me out on new adventures beyond my comfort zone, and then being there to hold my hand whenever things got scary. You are and continue to be the greatest blessing of my life.

And to my Savior and Lord Jesus Christ, who is the rock in my life, the foundation for this work, and the One who gives each of us a unique and beautiful purpose for our short time on this earth. I am forever grateful to Him for allowing me to share in the transformational good news: *that we can all experience lives that are On-Purpose.*

Wholehearted Purpose

Table of Contents

Foreword

Stories engage the heart and mind. *Wholehearted Purpose* uniquely captures the hearts of women's stories and displays the practical power of a 2-word purpose statement—as a simple spiritual and emotional anchor in the swirl and tossing of life and work. Each woman's story as included in this book offers insightful application for being On-Purpose.

The essential foundation of living On-Purpose involves knowing one's identity in Christ by way of one's unique 2-word purpose statement. Other than Christ, any other person, place, or thing is a counterfeit source of meaning. One's relationship and identity in Christ is mysterious. A purpose statement puts words on the intangible so the relationship can be more fully engaged, understood, and harnessed for everyday life—into eternity. On-Purpose is ultimately the best, most tested means I know to articulate one's identity in Christ and to bring it into expression.

As you read this compilation of women living On-Purpose, some stories will resonate more profoundly than others. Like inspirational gems in the jewelry box of your soul, store each story away for later use. Read and reread them to gain familiarity. Fresh insights will come with each reading. Much like a jewelry box, one day you may choose to "wear" another person's story of being on-purpose to inspire and guide you through your circumstance.

Within these pages, you will uncover a vulnerability and intimacy within each story. Secrets are shared. Challenges are faced and overcome. Life, death, and resurrection appear throughout these pages. As the song "Amazing Grace" so aptly recounts, you'll read of being lost—and being found. Along with these women, you'll endure hardships and rejoice in victories. I found real women dealing with real life counting on their real faith—even when it was as tiny in size as a mustard seed.

We're all "on-purpose persons" in creation. Having developed and worked with the concepts of On-Purpose since the late 1980s, I can tell you that being On-Purpose isn't easy—but I've yet to find a simpler or better way to go about living life. There isn't a day that goes by that I'm not learning some new dimension about the mysterious relationship and the role *purpose* plays to help us comprehend a new corner or cranny of the incomprehensible nature of God.

Knowing Mary Tomlinson as a business partner, friend, and sister in Christ, I knew this book would be one of Inspiring Hope—Mary's 2-word personal purpose. The world needs more people like Mary—solid in her convictions, tough and tender, diplomatic and directly honest, extraordinarily talented and delightfully cute, hardworking, and fun loving. I've watched Mary and Bill, her husband, lead worship services with songs of praise and thanksgiving; and I've worked side by side with her, doing deep strategy facilitation for corporations. I count our partnership a true blessing.

Mary is the coaches' coach. She's piloted the use of the On-Purpose Approach in a structured, one-on-one basis. When I meet Mary's clients, there's a consistent glint of joy and admiration for what she's done to enrich their lives.

On-Purpose is open to all and filled with those from many different traditions, ages, backgrounds, and experiences. Truly, come as you are; but expect a constant refinement and improvement in the manner in which you're leading your life as a follower of Christ.

For Men Only

Given the subtitle of this book, the target audience is clearly women. Men, do yourselves a favor and read these stories about God's gift to us of an ideal partner, or our helper (Genesis 2:18). The more we appreciate and accept women's unique perspective, the better we can appreciate and know God and who we are.

Glimpsing into so many women's lives through these easy-reading vignettes in such a brief time span provides multiple practical insights into the female psyche. Read this book as an intentional and loving act for the women in your life. Better yet, read one of the stories, and then ask your loved one what she thinks about it. Listen and learn, then love her unconditionally—as God has called us all to do.

Be On-Purpose!

Kevin W. McCarthy
Author of *The On-Purpose Person*
and *The On-Purpose Business Person*

Introduction

In 2013, my friend Julie called me on behalf of the newly formed Women Doing Well organization to ask if I would consider participating in a three-city pilot of one-day women's conferences called Inspiring Generous Joy. Women Doing Well had just completed the first ever research project on Christian women and their giving. The survey developers told them that they needed 300 women to complete the survey for it to be statistically significant and—just like our God—it became the largest ever research project on philanthropic giving with 7,336 women completing the survey.

One of the findings was that a strong sense of purpose leads to greater generosity—and women who know their purpose become more joyful, impactful givers.

Because of my passion and work with purpose, I was thrilled for the opportunity to participate sharing the On-Purpose message in the pilot cities of West Palm Beach, Houston, and Orlando. We all stepped out in faith and didn't know what God had in mind—but none of us ever dreamed of the dramatically positive response from those that attended.

Word spread, and we have now held the conference in thirteen cities. Additional cities are in the early planning stages. Sometimes when God moves, all you can do is hold on to His coattails and enjoy the ride.

The heart of the Inspiring Generous Joy Conference is to bring the tools that fit the hand of a woman to help her know her purpose, ignite her passion, and set her plan for giving to change the world.

These are the precious women who requested that I write this book. To be honest, at first I was unsure about how to tell the purpose story for women, but God has a way of continuing to invite us to join Him and take a step out of the boat. Although this book mirrors the same beautiful principles of *The On-Purpose Person* book, the difference is that it features women telling their own stories about finding their purpose.

On-Purpose Story Gathering

As I got started, I asked the Lord what He wanted to say to women through this book. His still small voice replied:

> *I have made each one of my daughters wonderfully and beautifully unique—no two are alike—each individually adored for who she is.*

> *I have tenderly created each one with a specific purpose and plan to reach the world in a way that she alone was designed to do.*

> *I am greatly pleased when my daughters discover and live out their divine purpose on earth, just as a loving Father would smile as He watches His daughter blossom into what she was always meant to be.*

Gathering these stories has been a joyful and surprising process. I was initially hesitant to approach women I had coached to contribute their stories. Some of these women I had coached more than ten years ago, and I thought perhaps with the passage of time, they would not remember their purpose or that it would not still be relevant in their lives. I didn't want to embarrass them—or myself! However, out of obedience, I did send the emails and the request because I knew that their stories could provide powerful encouragement from women who might be just like you.

Out of the thirty-six invitations, I had hoped to gather eight to ten stories. My ever encouraging husband said, "I think you will be surprised and will get more than twenty stories." Of course, I doubted him, and of course, he was right. Ultimately thirty-two brave, wonderful, and transparent women offered to share their purpose journeys with me and you as well. I personally knew most of them but some came from an invitation from the author of *The On-Purpose Person* himself—and I am so profoundly grateful.

The experience of reading their stories and what God had done in their lives became my own personal version of *It's a Wonderful Life*. As I was reading each story, I would have a smile on my face, a lump in my throat, and tears in my eyes. It was overwhelming to see how the seed of purpose had blossomed in their lives. I could see firsthand how the transformational power of this work was and is still very relevant and meaningful—even after all these years. I am deeply grateful for these brave women and their willingness to share their stories.

As I read each story, I made mental notes about what I knew about each woman—and I found that so many times I used the same words to describe each woman: I would say, "this woman is ... "

- Successful
- Smart

- Full of life
- In her own time of transition

I smiled at those who shared their initial skepticism of the process—remembering my own—and am grateful that all of us, despite our concerns, persevered through to the breakthroughs and transformation that we each discovered.

The stories you will read include women in all ages and walks of life, from—

- College age to empty-nesters.
- Stay-at-home moms to executive leaders.
- Single, divorced, or married women.

Their stories are encouraging, transparent, and refreshingly honest about the joys and struggles of seeking to live On-Purpose.

What is common with these stories, and with so many of us as women, is the fact that we can (and do) all appear completely successful on the outside. Those around us often automatically assume that we "have it all together."

The truth is that we all share doubts, uncertainties, and fears along with a deep desire to be all that God created us to be. But sometimes we can just get overwhelmed in the stuff of life. We lose our "way" because we have lost our "why."

Be encouraged as you read these women's stories in their own words; keep notes of your own reflections and know that God has a unique purpose for you!

The On-Purpose Framework

Life is so special and such a gift, to never unwrap the gift
is indeed a tragedy. — *Kevin W. McCarthy*

Background for the On-Purpose Message

How did On-Purpose come to be? If you ask Kevin W.
McCarthy, the author of *The On-Purpose Person*, he will
tell you that he discovered it rather than developed it!

Kevin is the ultimate entrepreneur and from an early age was
always looking for business opportunities and solutions. He
tells the story of being in eighth grade and negotiating the
first ever deal to sell Coca-Cola in the school cafeteria!

In his successful adult career he worked with and for a variety
of businesses and found that many businesses and their leaders
had ill-defined business plans and a lack of purpose—both
personally and professionally.

In his own personal life to gain clarity, he began by making
a list of goals for his life and work. With over 200 items, he
categorized them into the Life Accounts. Using his experience
as a tennis player and coach, he then used a Tournament

process to assess by pairs which of the two were the most important, advancing the winners to the next round and finally arriving at winners in each Life Account.

Solving the mystery of purpose, vision, mission, and values was another quest as the business books at the time did not adequately define these terms. His passion to bring clarity to these terms was created when he wrote *The On-Purpose Person* and *The On-Purpose Business Person* books over 20 years ago.

Kevin says about purpose:

> *Purpose is layman's language for expressing God's design and will—not as a relationship of works, but rather one of grace and presence. Your purpose statement is an outward expression and symbol to the depth and breadth of this mysterious relationship with God. As a result of articulating one's purpose, one is moved to align his or her life to one's purpose to become On-Purpose. Our purpose extends from God, in and through us in all we do, outward to those with whom we come in contact in the course of doing business and living life.*
>
> *The net result of living On-Purpose is an unconditional sense of blessing in the midst of either joy or suffering. It is knowledge of one's unique right to be and belong, plus a profound sense of love and significance, tempered by humbling acknowledgment of oneself relative to God. To know that one's life matters and makes a difference provides a solid and secure foundation to exercise free will wisely.*

Got Purpose?

As we begin the journey of finding purpose, there is a fundamental question that must first be discussed—what is your worldview?

If you believe as some do, that the world was created from a "big bang"—one incredible accident and subsequent random evolution—then the logic is that the universe and everything we see is an accident. Which means, you and I are also accidents in a randomly evolving world and there is no need to talk about our purpose.

But, if you believe that there is a design and a designer who thoughtfully created the universe, then everything has a specific design and a purpose including you and me. When we believe that we each have a specific design and a purpose, we can proceed on this exciting adventure to discover our unique design, which *is* our purpose.

To begin your own discovery, I find that we all intuitively know when we are on-purpose and off-purpose:

Think of two or three times in your own life when you were on-purpose—doing something that was easy and energizing. People commented on how well you did it, and time just flew. What were you doing?

_____

_____

_____

What are the words you would use to describe how it felt in those moments? Jot them down here.

_____

_____

_____

Typically, the words I hear around what it feels like to be on-purpose are *energizing, fulfilling, joyful, effortless,* and *content.*

Now, think of two or three times when you were off-purpose—times when whatever you were doing was hard or draining. You weren't particularly good at it, and time just dragged. What were you doing?

_____

_____

_____

What are the words you would use to describe how it felt in those moments?

_____

_____

_____

When I am leading a workshop and ask for the off-purpose words—they come fast and furious—we really know what off-purpose feels like! Some of the words I hear around what it feels like to be off-purpose are *draining, frustrating, tiring,* and *dry.*

Since we know what on- and off-purpose feel like, our goal then becomes: *how can we intentionally create more on-purpose moments in our lives and ensure less off-purpose moments?* Once we know our purpose, we can focus our efforts and energy on the things that are on-purpose!

On-Purpose Truths

Our purpose is permanent.

It's not as one woman said to me, "My purpose just went away to college." With a smile to encourage, I reminded her that she had a purpose before that child was born and after that child went away.

It is thrilling to think our Creator gave each of us a completely unique spiritual DNA, beautifully designed by the time we made our grand entrance to this earth. We came into this world prepackaged with our own sets of skills, gifts, talents, preferences, idiosyncrasies, and passions—and purpose. Psalm 139:13–15: *For you created my inmost being; you knit me together in my mother's womb. I praise you because I am fearfully and wonderfully made; your works are wonderful, I know that full well. My frame was not hidden from you when I was made in the secret place, when I was woven together in the depths of the earth.*

The work of discovering this design and our purpose is like being given a boxed jigsaw puzzle—without the box top which shows the picture of the completed puzzle. Our journey of discovering our purpose involves taking each puzzle piece about who we are, what we know, and what we've experienced out of the box, one at a time, to explore where it might fit. And, over time, as the individual pieces begin fitting together, the picture of our design and purpose will emerge.

Even our past (painful as it is at times) is a puzzle piece and fuels our passion for our purpose. Romans 8:28 states that "... *all things work for the good of those that love the Lord and are called according to His purpose.*" When we experience pain, a deep passion and empathy for others in similar circumstances can emerge. As a result, our painful experiences can ultimately drive our passion and commitment to live out our purpose, so that others do not have to experience the hurt that we have gone through. Romans 8:28 is my favorite verse because I love how God uses our personal pain to ultimately help others!

How to Use This Book

This book is designed to inspire you with stories of purpose and provide you with some of the basic tools to begin the discovery of your own purpose.

The stories of the women in this book came from their self-reflective work in an eight-week On-Purpose Person coaching program or time in workshops. I wish I could give you "three easy steps" to find your purpose, but this kind of work takes some commitment and reflective digging.

My hope is that their stories will encourage you and that this book will provide you with some thought-starters for your own On-Purpose journey. I pray you will be inspired by knowing that other women both struggle and find joy in discovering their personal design and purpose—and it is well worth the time and the energy to go through this process mindfully.

This book offers opportunities to apply and personalize the concepts. Throughout the book, after each woman's story, I will offer a "Purpose Facet." Each of these Purpose Facets includes a perspective offering a deeper view into your greater purpose.

Facets: Exploring Your Purpose Is Like Exploring a Diamond

Purpose is like the *facets* of a diamond or cut gem. The definition of facet is a particular aspect of something many-sided. Your unique purpose also has many facets—and they are each beautiful!

Each of the Purpose Facets in this book includes a perspective offering a deeper view into your greater purpose such as this:

PURPOSE FACET

The Great Commandment: "God, Self, and Others" is God's recurring order and theme. God writes desires on our hearts, has a plan for our lives, and fashions us to be His instruments of peace. Think about what you most want for others. One of the facets of our purpose is that what we most want for others is what we want for ourselves. As we live out our purpose for ourselves, our cup can then be filled by God to walk it out with others.

There will be a question after each story for your reflection and notes. Use your cumulative responses throughout the book as puzzle pieces for your own journey of discovery to see how God so beautifully designed you.

There are also resources at the back of the book to help you in your journey.

My prayer is that you will be inspired by these stories of women becoming On-Purpose, know just how incredibly unique YOU are, and discover your unique design to fill the needs of this world.

On-Purpose Definitions

In the following stories, you will see terms used in the On-Purpose coaching and training workshops. It will be helpful to understand these terms as you read their stories. They also may be useful as exercises for your own growth.

Want Lists, Tournaments, and Core Wants

We all experience static on the outside and static on the inside, and we can do something about the internal static. Knowing our purpose requires a thoughtful, reflective, and quiet mind and soul. To truly quiet our minds, we need to clear the internal static that so often shouts louder than the still soft voice of God. As multitasking women, there is always a running list in our heads of to-do's and "wants" that clamor for our attention and energy.

In the stories that follow, you will hear women talk about their Want Lists and Tournaments:

Want Lists

One of the best ways to clear the internal air is to honestly consider and write down what you want—right now—in each of the following life categories. Make a list for each category. They don't all have to be new ideas—it is OK to also list "I want to continue to ... "

- **Financial Wants**—Consider eliminating debt, increasing savings, buying a car, purchasing things you would like personally or for the house—think: "If I won the lottery, what would I buy?"

- **Physical, Health, and Recreational Wants**—think: "What would I like for my physical shape," "What would I like for my health," and for recreation—what is it you enjoy doing "just because"?

- **Spiritual Wants**—What do you want from God right now? What are the things that draw you closer to

Him? Try not to get too buried in all the lists of Christian activities such as teaching Sunday school but focus more on the things that truly bring you closer to Him.

- **Mental, Emotional, and Intellectual Wants**—What new things would you like to learn? What would you like to know more about? What types of things would challenge you intellectually? Consider any emotional issues you might want to address.

- **Family Wants**—Think first of each person in your immediate family individually and what you like in your relationship with them (note: there may be more than one want per person). Think of other extended family members individually and what you want to happen or do with them. Consider family wants as a whole—such as holding a reunion, taking a family photo, or engaging in family dinners.

- **Vocational/Career Wants**—What are the attributes of work that you most love? What is important to you in your work? If you were designing the perfect job for yourself, what would you include?

- **Social and Community Wants**—Think of what you want with your friends (think of specific friends and what you want with each of them). Think of current or past friends to reconnect with. Think of social activities—such as a dinner club. Think of community groups to be involved with (or continue) that keep you connected with others.

- **Giving Wants**—What are all the volunteer opportunities or ways to give back that you might have? Think of giving of your time, talent, and treasure.

In this process, it is important that you allow yourself to be honest and dream. This is not about editing yourself by saying: *I know I want this, but it is impossible or silly, so I won't write it down.* It's really important that if you want it, it gets written down.

For those who might hesitate thinking we as Christians should not have any wants, I would like to remind you of Psalm 37:4: *Delight yourself in the Lord and He will give you the desires of your heart.* He already knows the desires that are in our hearts, so we might as well come clean and put them down on paper!

Tournaments

Once the Wants Lists are compiled by category, we can run "Tournaments" (think NCAA March Madness brackets or a tennis tournament). A free resource is included on page 173. The process is this:

- Look at each category individually (such as Financial), and of the 8 or 16 Wants listed, consider them in pairs of two (like Two Teams Competing), and of the two, choose and advance the one that is more important to you. For example: between number 1 and number 2 on my list—which is more important to me right now?
- Continue the process two by two until you have a Core Want in each category.

Top Want

You will also hear from women in the following stories who identified their most important want—which sometimes surprised them.

This process works once you have a winner in each of your eight life categories. Get out another sheet of paper—number it from 1 to 8 and write down your top wants in each of the categories. Run another Tournament (again asking the question, *What is most important to me?*) to identify the single most important Top Want in your life right now.

The Top Want winner reveals total clarity of your top priority. So even if you have twenty-five things on your "to do" list today—you now know what is currently your single most important want.

Knowing what is most important diminishes the noise of some of our less important wants. It's great to repeat the process on an annual basis (on your birthday or at the end of the year) as you will find that your most important wants will likely change over time. For example, what I wanted in my relationship with my children ten years ago is different from what I want today. And what I want physically is definitely different from 10 years ago! The exercise is a clarifying one as you will see in the stories that follow.

The Terms "Purpose," "Vision," "Mission," "Values"

If I were to ask 10 people on the street how they define the above terms, I am certain I would receive 10 different answers.

In an On-Purpose context, we define these words as follows:

Purpose Answers the Question: "Why Do I Exist?"

Purpose answers the heart questions of "why do I exist?" or "who am I uniquely in Christ?" The On-Purpose Approach narrows this down to two words to get to the true soul core (and to make it easy to remember). Because of the depth of this soulful search, it is not a simple process but one that requires reflective and prayerful time.

In this book, along with the stories about purpose, questions will be provided to begin to discover your meaningful 2-word purpose statement. In the Resources section, there is mention of a website to enable you to explore purpose after you have done your reflective work. The simplicity of a 2-word statement allows us to remember and be mindful of our purpose at all times.

Ways to explore your purpose statement include taking quiet moments to:

- Consider those two to three times in your life when you were on-purpose and off-purpose. What is in common with your on-purpose moments and what is in common when you are off-purpose?

- Write out the story of your life and pay particular attention to those defining moments when— whatever was happening at the time—made a profound impact on who you are today. Sometimes defining moments are wonderfully positive and other times tragic and painful but they are part of who YOU are.

- Think about what you most want for others—if you were to meet with someone for coffee and after the meeting, I would ask you what you most want for that individual—what would you say?

Ultimately, by discovering your 2-word purpose statement:

- You will be able to align your life and choices to ensure more on-purpose moments.

- You will more quickly be able to discern when and why you are off-purpose.

- You will be able to get back on-purpose more quickly by running back to Father God—the one who created you.

- You will live your purpose in all aspects of life: at home, with your spouse and children, at work, at church, in your community, and with your friends.

- And most importantly, you will change your world by living out what God has always designed you to be.

Purpose Facet

Discovering your purpose is like the beautiful struggle of a caterpillar becoming a butterfly. I will provide tools to help your thinking, but I want you to know that getting to the core of your God-given purpose is not something where you can snap your fingers and instantly know your unique purpose. Although it may be tempting to "cut the caterpillar cocoon" to expedite the process for the emerging butterfly, we know that when someone tries to free the butterfly and eliminate the struggle, the butterfly will die because her wings have not been made strong during the emerging process. Be encouraged that clarity is achievable, but be willing to work for it as the women in the following stories have demonstrated.

Vision Answers—Where Am I Going?

Vision involves the eyes and head as we think and envision. I am always amazed at how few people ever consider where they want to be in ten years. We all busily go through life and before we know it, another ten years have passed. Sadly many of us are victims to what the Cheshire Cat in *Alice in*

Wonderland says, "If you don't know where you are going, any road will get you there."

Having an articulated vision of where we want to go guides us as we choose the roads that will get us there (and discern which roads will get us off track). We need to regularly revisit our vision and seek the Lord's anointing—but I also say, "*God cannot steer a parked car.*" I have found that I need to pray, plan, and move forward putting the car in gear trusting that He will guide and direct my life car.

- Envision and write your desired future. Ask: *what would I like my life to look like ten years from today?*

_____

_____

_____

_____

Missions Answer—How Will I Get There?

"Missions" refer to the hands and feet that make things happen. Our definition is that it becomes the "how" to achieving the vision—the practical steps to achieve what you have envisioned.

- What are the three to five things that must happen in order for your 10-year vision to be achieved?

_____

_____

_____

_____

_____

Values Answer—What Is Most Important to Me Along the Way?

The definition of values is *a person's principles or standards of behavior; one's judgment of what is important in life.* Values are not right or wrong and it will help us to remember that others may not share our values. One person may have a high value of patriotism and another does not, or someone may value promptness and others do not.

Our values reflect what is deeply important to us, and we gain clarity by knowing and being able to state our values. If we or someone else violates a value that is important to us, we will experience a physical reaction such as "I felt sick to my stomach" or "I had a bad gut feeling about this."

- What are your five core values? Think of those things that when you or someone else violates those values, you feel a pit in your stomach.

_____

_____

_____

_____

_____

"In Him we were also chosen, having been predestined according to the plan of Him who works out everything in conformity with the purpose of His will."—Ephesians 1:11

NOTES

_____

_____

_____

_____

_____

_____

_____

_____

_____

_____

_____

_____

_____

My Story:
From Disney to Inspiring Hope

I guess it is only fair that if these women were vulnerable enough to share their story that I should start with mine. I'll begin with how I became so passionate about helping others find their purpose—and then share the more intimate details of my own purpose discovery.

Before I met Kevin W. McCarthy, the author of the powerful message of On-Purpose, I enjoyed an eighteen-year corporate career with Disney and had the privilege and blessing of managing talented teams of eight to eight hundred people. I found it interesting that often these same talented individuals would come sit in my office and sadly confess that they *just weren't happy in their work* or that it *wasn't the "right fit" for them.* They had dreams and passions of doing other things but were stuck and unsure how to move ahead. *How could they discover what they were really made to do?* I didn't know it then, but I was encountering hearts that were simply off-purpose.

Not only was I experiencing off-purpose hearts but from a business branding perspective, Disney's theme park Epcot had just opened and we began the process of branding. We spent months identifying the core unique aspects and positioning of each product to clearly differentiate each park—knowing that more major theme parks were planned. We were applying the same principles of purpose, vision, mission, and values for a business.

It became very clear that whether I was branding a business or trying to understand the brand of an individual, getting to the core essence was key—but I hadn't met Kevin W. McCarthy yet, and we didn't call it purpose.

After 18 years at Disney, in 2001 I felt the Lord call me to leave Disney and start my own business. He made it clear that it was time to leave, but, as is often with the Lord, He was less clear about what I was to do next. At the time, this was a true leap of faith considering I had no real business plan and two teenagers getting ready for college. From a practical bottom-line perspective, it was not the most logical time to take a jump into the unknown, so I knew it had to be God and I knew He was calling me to step out in faith.

In the first couple of months after Disney, a friend of mine asked what I wanted to do, and I said, "I'm not totally sure, but I think I would love to consult, coach, and speak."

He said, "Then, you need to meet my friend, Kevin. He's been doing those things for more than twenty years." My first thought was, *if anyone has been doing this kind of work for more than twenty years and is successful—I want to meet that person!*

With a little research before we met, I found that he had written two successful books—*The On-Purpose Person* and *The On-Purpose Business Person*—which I read. I was amazed that Kevin's concepts of purpose, vision, mission, and values were essentially the same concepts our Disney team used in the business branding work we had done and also perfectly described the needs that were being addressed in those informal coaching sessions in my office with my staff and coworkers searching for right fit.

Kevin and I met, found our similarities in a love for God and a passion for purpose for business and individuals, and thus began an exciting journey of being partners and champions of On-Purpose. We worked together for several years, and then I launched my own On-Purpose Partners business to share the importance of purpose with organizations and individuals.

Although my consulting business includes many other workplace issues—such as customer service, team building, and leadership—my heart is most alive when I am working with individuals to find their God-given purpose. In my On-Purpose coaching work and workshops, I get a front row seat to experience the heart cry of those who desperately want to know that they HAVE a purpose and that they CAN lead fulfilled and giving lives.

Mary

exists to serve by **Inspiring Hope**

In-spir-ing: Making somebody feel more enthusiastic, confident, or stimulated; generating creativity or enthusiasm. Stirring, rousing, moving, exciting, stimulating.

Hope: A feeling of expectation and desire for a certain thing to happen. Grounds for believing that something good may happen. Optimism, expectation, expectancy, desire, and anticipation.

My own personal story—like all of ours—begins with an honest look back over my life to find clues of my purpose.

My life started with what appeared to be a loving church-going family with parents that never fought. Sadly, I did not know that this was falsely idyllic for much of my first 10 years. But that all changed the summer of my eleventh year.

I can still remember that hot, carefree summer day at my home, giggling and running through the sprinklers with my friends, when my dad came home with a concerned look on his face and told me that my friends needed to go home. We took a walk, and he told me that my mother was leaving him. I broke down in tears, and he suggested going for ice cream to help lighten the mood.

On that simple trip for ice cream, in what unfolded as a bizarre set of circumstances, I became an unwilling passenger in a frightening three-car chase through our small town, as my father (with me in the car) gave chase to my mother (who had my sister in her car) with another man in a third car. At one stoplight, my mother's car got through before the light turned red, but my father's and the other man's cars were stopped. Dad jumped out of our car and a fistfight broke out between my father and the other man in the middle of the intersection as I helplessly watched this terrifying scene in front of me. I was scared and deeply hurt as I watched people slow down to stare without offering to help. After the police arrived and sorted things out and we went back to the house, it was now just Dad and me—both of us silently mourning the life-changing events of that day.

In the weeks and months that followed, I remember many tearful nights sitting in my bed as I wondered why God had let this happen. This new life with just Dad and me was an adjustment, especially for him trying to understand the emotions and needs of a pre-teen girl. He had to help me buy my first bra (both of us thankful for sales ladies back then to help me in the dressing room) and navigate the emotions and embarrassment around my first menstrual period.

After a couple of years, I believed I was adjusting to our new normal, until one day, my mother unexpectedly showed up at my house unrecognizable at first in a blonde wig. There was another man (her lawyer) with her and after the promise of a short ride to get reacquainted with Mom, I was kidnapped that day as they took me across the country against my will. She called my Dad to assure him that I was with her and over the next weeks and months, as my parents sorted out next steps, they decided it would be best for my sister and me to spend school years with Mom and summers with Dad.

It was awkward being with both my mom and sister again.

The "other man" in the car chase scene was now her husband. He frightened me with his drinking, loud dish-breaking arguments, and physical abuse of my mother. None of this made sense to me. I constantly asked the old proverbial question, "If God is good, why do bad things happen to good people?" My version of God was a strict judgmental and uninvolved God and I wasn't so sure I wanted anything to do with Him.

In high school, I met some friends who shared that God was really a loving Father—one who had been beside me every day, had shared my pain and cried with me over what had happened, and who had a plan for my life. I came to know Christ as my Savior as a teenager, and He held me close during those difficult teenage years.

After high school, I thought college, a career, and marriage would provide the escape I needed, but I often felt void of joy, full of despair, and stuck in a rut for days, weeks, or months. It was hard to know what was causing it or how to get out of it. I would just hold on, hoping that it would eventually pass and I would feel better again. I know now how off-purpose I was, but I didn't have the words for it then.

I met and married Bill within nine months of our first date. He was strong, patient, and comforting to me and for the first time in a long time, I felt safe. But after three struggling years in our early marriage with my own ongoing, unceasing search for identify and meaning, we decided the only answer was to divorce. We determined that the next logical step was for one of us to move out. However, since apartments were expensive, and I was working days and he was working nights, we decided we could live platonically at opposite ends of the house as we worked through the details of the divorce. I remember exchanging a cordial hello to each other each morning as I would leave the house for work, and he would be coming home from the night shift and hand me the morning paper.

I was seeing a counselor at the time, and a Marriage Encounter Retreat was suggested. Figuring Bill and I had nothing to lose, we decided to go and it allowed us each to do a lot of journaling and sharing about our feelings. Miraculously and mysteriously on that weekend, God began very slowly and gently to mend our broken hearts and our broken marriage. God kept us together by a thread during those days, and I am forever grateful, because today our marriage has never been better.

Fast forward, my next twenty-five years were filled with a demanding work career, worldwide travel, and two wonderful children. After 18 years at Disney (and wonderful stories—perhaps another book?), it was 2001 when I stepped away from my Disney career and met Kevin W. McCarthy—and personally experienced the On-Purpose Person Process.

Going through the On Purpose Person Process, I reflected back on the moments in my life when I felt most "on-purpose."—when I was doing something I felt I was *made to do.* On my lists were motivating and leading a team in high school to design and build a homecoming float, tackling big problems at work, getting teams to move forward, and simply listening to someone share a personal story and being able to provide perspective. Those were all moments that I felt alive.

Conversely, when I reflected back on times when I was "off-purpose"—I was unable to motivate myself or others, experienced despair about my marriage, and felt trapped with perpetually negative people or doing work that was maintenance rather than solution or improvement focused.

As I reflected, wrote, and prayed through the On-Purpose Person Process, I was equally excited and a little nervous about the possibility of discovering my 2-word purpose statement. What if it was wrong? What if it sent me in the wrong direction? What if it were not really possible to discover who God created me to be?

As is often the case with those I have worked with over the years, it was hard for me to discover my 2-word purpose alone. I think we are just too close to ourselves to see ourselves as clearly as others and God see us. When Kevin suggested that my purpose statement was "Inspiring Hope," I honestly wasn't as sure at first. It seemed aspirational, but the simplicity of it scared me. Was that my core purpose? And truthfully, part of my skepticism was knowing just how often I would do and feel the absolute opposite!

He suggested that I ask those who knew and loved me the most for their thoughts—and their responses surprised me. "Well of COURSE that is your purpose statement!" "Absolutely!" were the responses.

So, despite my tentative acceptance, I agreed to live with it for a while and walk it out day by day. I found that in the moments when I really felt on-purpose—at work, with a friend, with my family—I realized I truly was Inspiring Hope—and in the moments I felt most off-purpose, I was not at all inspiring or hopeful but instead feeling despair and a sense of *hopelessness*.

Knowing my purpose also brought another life-changing insight. Whenever I would think, say, or do something that was not on-purpose, I would feel an instant conviction internally in my spirit, saying things like, "Now that thought was *not* Inspiring Hope," or "Those words you just spoke were *certainly not* Inspiring Hope" Ouch! Knowing my purpose sure held me accountable!

Another wonderful on-purpose outcome was that whenever I felt off-purpose (as we all do), instead of stewing in a funk for hours, days, or weeks (or longer), I could more quickly identify that this was simply an off-purpose moment, and I could get back on-purpose quickly. Each time, and to this day, when I feel off-purpose, I go back to the One who created me and tell Him that I am not feeling on-purpose, and I need Him to once again Inspire Hope in me, so that I can Inspire Hope in myself and ultimately in others. This process gets me back on track to being on-purpose so much more quickly than the days prior to knowing my purpose statement.

Over the years as I have walked out this purpose statement, which was at first a bit of a stranger to me, I have come to know with absolute surety that this is the purpose God has for me while I am on the face of this earth. Having the knowledge of one's purpose brings great accountability. I can no longer say, "Well, Lord, I just didn't know my purpose."

As one of the women you will read about said, "It's not a one and done process; it must be constantly nurtured, explored, and offered to the Lord." I wholeheartedly agree and hope you will enjoy your own process of becoming an On-Purpose Woman—because as you know, I want to be on-purpose and Inspire Hope in you!

Purpose Facet

Purpose brings clarity and focus. I believe many of us live our lives a bit out of focus—with a lack of understanding of why things have happened (and are happening) to us. Similar to looking through a camera lens that needs only a slight adjustment to bring the picture into full beauty and clarity—with purpose, when you see the true picture of your life, it is joyful and beautiful!

Like the camera analogy, is there anything out of focus in your life today?

On-Purpose Reflections

On-Purpose Stories

In Times of Transition

Know who you really are ...
make plans for who you can become.

When life gets complicated and we are in the midst of change, we can lose our way and identity. Things we were once sure about become fuzzy, and we have to rebalance and rediscover our identity once again.

Reestablishing our priorities and how we can stay grounded in our purpose enables us to weather the storms of change.

Let's get started with our On-Purpose women stories! I am excited to introduce you to each one of these amazing women. If any of their stories stir something deep within you and you would like to connect further, just send me a note at *mary@marytomlinson.com*.

Linda

exists to serve by **Instilling Confidence**

In-still-ing: To impress ideas, principles, or teachings gradually on somebody's mind. Inspire, fill, encourage, infuse, introduce.

Con-fi-dence: Self-assurance or a belief in your ability to succeed; belief or trust in somebody or something or in the ability of somebody or something to act in a proper, trustworthy, or reliable manner; a relationship based on trust and intimacy. Self-assurance, poise, trust, support, loyalty, conviction, certainty.

Introducing Linda

During my career, I had the privilege to work for wonderful leaders—one of whom was Linda! She led our division through many exciting times with grace and a steady hand. Now that she is retired, she has continued to fulfill God's purpose in her life with her family and those around her. So thankful for the leaders in my life that God has used to shape me!

My On-Purpose Person work came at exactly the right time in my life—and during a time of great transition.

My mother, the rock of our family, had recently passed, and

I was in a period of intense grieving over our loss. I had also left a Fortune 100 Company as a senior executive and wanted to sort out my next steps.

My 2-word purpose statement is to Instill Confidence. Not surprisingly, this is exactly what my mother did for me all my life! Since doing this important work with Mary in 2010, I now go into situations focusing on Instilling Confidence in all of those with whom I come into contact—by encouraging, inspiring, and building them (and the team) up.

This purpose work revealed to me that I was not entering into all situations with my purpose at the forefront of my mind. As an executive at a large, dynamic company, there were many competing forces at work. Instead of a positive attitude (which was my natural response), I was faced with a leader whose leadership style was not necessarily on-purpose for me. I saw firsthand how a leader at cross-purposes impacts the team. Being on-purpose and staying on-purpose is now always my goal.

And despite the important moments of clarity with the On-Purpose Person Process, I have found that this purpose work is not a "one and done" type discovery. It needs to be revisited often and reflected upon as life and demands change.

Today, I know my Top Wants include taking care of my father, being very involved in the Bible Study Fellowship Group, and working part-time helping businesses transition their marketing organizations and customer experience processes.

Life continues to evolve and change—but reviewing the purpose work frequently inspires me and reminds me of what I need to do to be and stay on-purpose!

Purpose Facet

Looking back over your past helps you find some of the puzzle pieces to identifying the image of your purpose. Being on-purpose has a 360-degree impact—how can you be on-purpose every day with yourself, with your family, at work, with your friends, and in your community? And as you reflect, may you also be grateful for those in your life who have nurtured your purpose along the way.

Who in your life has nurtured you to know who God made you to be? What about them most inspired you?

On-Purpose Reflections

_____

_____

_____

$\mathcal{A}nna$

exists to serve by **Liberating Freedom**

Lib-er-at-ing: To set somebody free from constraints. Release, set free, unshackle, unfetter, energizing, invigorating.

Free-dom: A state in which somebody is able to act and live as he or she chooses, without being subject to any undue restraints or restriction; ease of movement; openness and friendliness in speech or behavior. Liberty, independence, choice, nonconformity, abandon, candor.

Introducing Anna

When we were in Orlando, I met Anna as the fun and lively wife of one of our clergy at church. With her prior life as a lawyer, she was smart and accomplished—a woman who seemed to have it all together! Now that my daughter has married a pastor, I have a new appreciation of the challenges of being a pastor's wife and balancing many plates all at once. In addition to her clergy wife role, Anna has five children—so you know THIS woman lives a busy life!

When I was invited to contribute to this book, I was delighted to have a "legitimate" reason to revisit my on-purpose journey. I began the on-purpose journey as a midlife reality check. I was at a crossroads in all areas of my life. With five children, a clergy husband, and a need and desire to return to work and rebuild my professional life, I wanted to start from a blank slate.

Not surprisingly, my schedule at that time was crisis-driven. I also knew that we were going to be relocating for a new call to a different church, but I had no idea of where, when, or a host of other unknowns. If I didn't figure out some sort of plan for myself in the midst of all these changes, nothing would happen for me.

As I look back on almost two years of on-purpose living, I still feel like I am walking on an unfinished bridge; but being on-purpose helps me build a sound structure for that bridge. I have a framework in my life and a process to follow when life happens. When stuck, I ask myself, *how can I live my purpose of Liberating Freedom?*

To manage being in a fast-paced, demanding, reactive season, one of the best ways I Liberate Freedom for myself is by looking to the function of being on-purpose. Early on in the process, after some trial and error, I discovered the snooze button on my alarm. Now, to Liberate Freedom for myself, I set my alarm fifteen minutes earlier than when I need to get up. I hit snooze and quietly spend the next twelve minutes thinking and prioritizing my day. No one bugs me or asks me to focus on something else. My husband asked me why I don't just set my clock later instead of hitting snooze. I laughed as I realized that my dastardly plan had worked. I have my own uninterrupted planning time at a very useful part of my day.

By thinking through my priorities before my feet hit the floor, I can accomplish the most important stuff each day. My core wants have remained the same over the past two years. Yet, as the details change, I feel more focused on what is important.

The framework of my purpose statement, Liberating Freedom, which can flow easily through my life, makes decisions easier.

If something doesn't hang on my core wants, then it is not high on my priority list. I can still do a lot of things, but I am clearer about the truly important tasks.

There is a joy in living which I don't want to miss due to being mired in minutiae. I still struggle to stay on-purpose some days. I remain a work in progress. However, I know on most days, I have spent my time in a meaningful way. There still are many days when I dangle from the cables on that unfinished bridge, but I can see the framework filling up solidly and steadily to living a life on-purpose. And of course in honor of my purpose statement of Liberating Freedom, every once in a while I just dangle from those cables and enjoy the view.

Purpose Facet

Being on-purpose is a lifelong journey that's practical and fun. We're truly on-purpose persons co-creating with God our designer.

When was a time when you were on-purpose and it was fun?

On-Purpose Reflections

_____

_____

_____

Leslie

exists to serve by **Stimulating Significance**

Stim-u-lat-ing: Encourage something, make somebody interested in or excited about something, make somebody more alert. Inspiring, motivating, exciting, thought-provoking, refreshing, energizing, rousing.

Sig-nif-i-cance: The quality of having importance or being regarded as having great meaning. Worth, consequence, impact, importance, magnitude, substance.

Introducing Leslie

If you were to ask anyone who knows Leslie, they would all say that they have never seen her without a huge smile on her face. This woman exudes joy! Her life looked picture perfect from the outside—a successful doctor husband, beautiful and smart children, and her life of volunteer service to the community and the church. Her story is such a beautiful illustration that taking some time to reflect on who we are and what is most important may be standing right in front of us!

I chose to go through the On-Purpose Person coaching when our second child was a senior in high school. I had worked full time until our second child was two years old, but then I stepped away from paid employment and volunteered full time in our children's activities, major civic roles, and substantial leadership roles at our church. I organized large ski trips for the school, led 160 high school choir students to Carnegie Hall, ran the high school band trip for 190 students to the Fiesta Bowl, and kept the house running for a family of four with a physician husband who was not home much. My list of leadership roles went on and on.

Our oldest child was going to graduate school and was an accomplished young woman set on her own path, and our son was graduating from high school. It was time for me. I needed to figure out who I was and what my personal life would look like in the near future. I did not want to "crash and burn" as my life changed from being a full-time mother to having no children at home. Now what? I was panicked. I knew Mary Tomlinson and Kevin W. McCarthy personally and was aware of their work and the coaching process.

I was going to start the process when our son went to college in the fall, but he told me, "Mom, get started before you fall apart. I cannot worry about you when I am in college. You need your own life." He was right, and I started the process the spring of his senior year.

The end result of my work around the tournaments and what was most important to me shocked me so much, I could not tell anyone for weeks. I had to absorb it myself first. My final most important want was "To stay married to my husband." We had been married for twenty-four years at this time, raised two very accomplished children, lived a life with no financial worries, had loving parents and many personal friends we adored, and enjoyed an extremely active travel life and holidays spent with family and friends. Our life was picture perfect on the outside, yet our marriage needed new fuel. We had grown apart due to the demands of his profession, raising two children, and my civic responsibilities. We "had it all"—yet lacked emotional love and attachment to each other. Living apart and starting anew had started looking attractive—as well as finding true emotional love.

Staying married as my number one want was so surprising and shocking to me that it took me weeks to share this news with my husband. I was embarrassed, feeling helpless and overwhelmed. *How do I stay married?* I contemplated.

This process made me focus on our relationship and how to make it centered on God. It is hard work to be married, and yet I discovered that each day has brought a new chance to honor my spouse, support him, and uphold our marriage.

We just celebrated our thirtieth wedding anniversary, and my marriage has taken the front seat in my life. After my relationship with God, my husband and our time together comes first. We now try to be the best role models of a married couple that we can be for our children. When our marriage is not at its finest, I remind myself of my number one want—and keep on going.

A collage I made during my On-Purpose sessions hangs next to my computer. At the top of the collage, it says "I love George," and next to it is a picture of us with "rekindle an old flame" written below the picture. I look at this collage five to ten times a day as a reminder of how I want to live my life:

Stimulating Significance is my 2-word purpose statement. Honestly, at first I didn't see myself this way. But the definitions of these two words really do describe me: activate, excite, produce an action, positive energy, stimulate the heart, turn something that may not be working into a positive, do things in life with tremendous value and depth, have a meaningful life, be decisive, determining, relevant, and useful.

My life has always included verbally thanking people, telling people how much I appreciate them and their work, complimenting people, sending all kinds of greeting cards: sympathy, birthday, congratulation, graduation, or get well. I call people on the phone just to say hello, and I send daily emails of love to my mother and my two out-of-town children. I have always done this. After completing the On-Purpose Person Process, I make a point of doing it even more. I carve out an hour a week now to telephone a friend, send cards, write friendship emails, or arrange a coffee time with someone who is on my heart. I now send our children texts daily with words of love, and I email them. If I miss a day, they follow up and want to make sure everything is okay.

As I volunteer at the local children's hospital, I am intentional about stopping to chat with the janitors, employees cleaning hospital rooms, receptionists, cafeteria workers, security guards, nurses, and physicians. Each employee is important, and I can remind them of that just by stopping and sharing a few kind, loving words. Hospitals are busy, hectic places focusing on the healing of patients. I take the time to focus on those who are healing others, and I know I glow when I am Stimulating Significance.

To ensure that I am being intentional, at the beginning of each month I now make a list of people I want to call or spend time with that month. Some folks I see in person, some I call, some I have "phone tea" with (we arrange a time to talk and each sip hot tea while we telephone talk), or some I sit with at church. Maintaining friendships takes time, focus, and energy. When I am Stimulating Significance, I am on-purpose. I am thankful this process has helped me to realize this!

Staying on-purpose is a daily challenge due to the fast-paced society we live in with the influence of technology, the pressures of life, and the global challenges of the world. Life is ever changing, and so are we. Since the start of my On-Purpose Person Process in the fall of 2009, I have done the Tournament process two more times. I will find a few hours and reread the last tournament list and values list, and check with myself as to how I am doing.

At my desk hangs the collage I made in 2009 with my values and top wants. In the front of my monthly/weekly planner is a typed list of my top wants. I find myself reading the lists in the planner on airplanes and in hotel rooms when I have a few quiet moments to reflect.

I continued to work toward my Tournament Wants. Here is a list of my wants—with updates for each in italics:

Financial: Get a different house or different space in our current home. *This will be the year of remodeling our current house and I have discontinued two volunteer positions to make this the number one activity.*

Physical/Recreational: Lose weight. *I did lose twenty pounds and have kept it off. It is a daily decision to maintain my current weight. Staying at my current weight is a daily challenge, and I would still like to lose five more pounds. I go to the gym five days a week and eat low-fat, low-carb food, which is a daily challenge.*

Spiritual: Get quiet, and listen to God. *Until 2014, I was doing a very bad job at this. I wanted to change, but had not. In 2014, a spiritual leader at our church approached me about being a "Centering Prayer Leader." I felt as if God handed this one to me on a silver platter, and I am now worshiping one to two times a week at our church in a quiet form of prayer—listening to God. My husband and I attend a Celtic quiet service on Sunday nights together, and this is rewarding for both of us and strengthens our marriage. It is a daily challenge for me to "get quiet and listen to God," yet I am working on it and growing.*

Intellectual: Learn Apple computer. *I have attacked the most recent iPhone and a new Apple computer, but there is still room for growth. I could use more work here and want to acquire more technology skills.*

Family: Find things the four of us can do together. *We are now a family of five (our daughter married a wonderful man), and I am very intentional about planning trips we can all go on with activities we can all enjoy and share. Living in three different states requires careful holiday planning, detailed trip planning, and intentional time securing activities we all want to do and enjoy when we are together. We are doing very well with this!*

Vocation: Become a hospital chaplain. *I am now a volunteer hospital chaplain and love it. I volunteer weekly. When doors open, I attend additional training, conferences, workshops, and hospital activities. I am called and on-purpose when I am at* the hospital! For me, it is an honor to do God's work in a children's hospital.

Social: Get social dinner group started. *I have not done this and would still like to do so. I go through stages where I am better about arranging group social activities than others.*

Husband: Stay married to George. *I remain intentional about this number one core want, and when there are times when the marriage is stretched to the max, I remind myself of this. This requires constant work, and there is a lot of room for growth as our chapters in life change.*

My insights into this process are that it is ongoing and takes time and constant effort; the efforts are worth their weight in gold. Living on-purpose is a choice and decision. I am happier, have a sense of constant direction, and never thirst for goals. I feel my family, friends, and community benefit from me being on-purpose. The process of Tournaments and Core Wants is easy to accomplish, and I would like to do it yearly. I have decided to live on-purpose forever.

PURPOSE FACET

Psalm 37:4 says, "Take delight in the Lord, and he will give you the desires of your heart." Being on-purpose helps you identify what is most important in your life right now. Rather than the noisy busyness of your mind and heart with the chorus of "all the things I have to do"—you can know and be intentional about what is most important right now—and find joy in the focus.

What are the three most important things in your life right now?

ON-PURPOSE REFLECTIONS

_____

_____

_____

Kathy

exists to serve by **Nurturing Belief**

Nur-tur-ing: To give tender care and protection to encourage somebody or something to grow, develop, thrive, and be successful; to keep a feeling in the mind for a long time, allowing it to grow or deepen. Care for, raise, foster, cultivate, develop, cherish, support, encourage.

Be-lief: Acceptance by the mind that something is true or real, often underpinned by an emotional or spiritual sense of certainty; confidence that somebody or something is good or will be effective; faith in God. Faith, conviction, confidence, trust, certainty.

Introducing Kathy

My dear friend Kathy I have known since our college days when she and I were in a singing group called Variations. Our husbands were very good friends and would tease each other and dream about the next "get rich" pyramid scheme—all in good fun. We stayed in touch over the years, and none of us were prepared when we heard that Kathy's husband had died by suicide.

When I was introduced to the On-Purpose Person Process, my father had just passed away—and I was recently empty-nested, menopausal, and struggling in my job. I was also still dealing with the grief of my ex-husband's death—who, after twenty years of marriage and eight weeks after our divorce, died by suicide. Needless to say, I didn't know what I wanted, didn't know who I was, and just felt I was floundering after going through all these life changes.

I started the On-Purpose Person Process rather skeptical, to be honest. It was ironic, because the process starts with developing Want Lists, and I had no CLUE what I wanted. So many years had been built around my family, spouse, and job that I hadn't taken the time to think of what I wanted. A Want List was so foreign to me. It took a lot of work to start dreaming again ... but it was so worth it. Once I allowed myself to let go and imagine again—it actually became fun! Then, it got really interesting—when I had to narrow down those wants to the most important to me at the time. Of all the categories, my most important want was my son's salvation, which prompted an important decision to find the right time and place to talk to him about the Lord and his feelings. What a powerful moment!

The process is cathartic and involves hard work, and yet at the same time, it's energizing and powerful. It almost feels as if you're giving birth to a "new you." My 2-word purpose statement was a struggle. In fact I didn't want to accept the 2-word purpose statement Mary suggested and laughed when it boiled down to Nurturing Belief. *Me?* The one who had such a hard time with my own belief? But I so dearly loved to nurture belief in others. To this day, I can tell when I have Nurtured Belief in someone, when that wonderful, sweet peace comes over me. I always think about being on-purpose in that moment, and I am grateful.

Prior to this work, I found that so much of my effort to Nurture Belief involved me trying to force it. I realized that when I rely on God and allow HIM to take control (and relinquish my own need for control), that my purpose truly comes alive. To be honest, I still struggle from time to time with accepting that I am to Nurture Belief, but I have come to realize that my purpose statement can only truly be fulfilled when I am focused on God and not myself.

I keep the On-Purpose study guide in my nightstand, and from time to time take a look at it. Some of the goals are met; others have changed. It definitely was one of the most precious times in my life—to come out on the other side of the process and feel like I knew where I was going and what I was supposed to be doing. It's funny how many people find it hard to believe that you can KNOW your purpose. But I say, "It's a God thing," and believe after going through this process that you CAN know your purpose.

Purpose Facet

You know you have a good purpose statement when you can take each word of your purpose statement, and flip it to the negative, and it pierces your heart. Your own life experiences deeply connect with those negative counterparts and you know those negative feelings. Your pain in knowing the opposite of your purpose statement drives your passion to be on-purpose. When you know that you personally need your purpose statement in your OWN life, it is a good purpose statement.

What is it you most want for other people—that you also need for yourself?

ON-PURPOSE REFLECTIONS

_____

_____

_____

Judy

exists to serve by **Embracing Significance**

Em-brac-ing: Welcome eagerly or willingly; to hug someone; to adopt or take up something, especially a belief or way of life; to surround or enclose something. Hold close, grip, accept, welcome, adopt, support, include, involve.

Sig-nif-i-cance: The quality of having importance or being regarded as having great meaning. Worth, consequence, impact, importance, magnitude, substance.

Introducing Judy

One of the precious women I have met through the Women Doing Well organization is Judy. Gracious, loving, and fun, she has dedicated her working life to the Lord with Campus Crusade for Christ (CRU). Big and wonderful changes all came at once for Judy as you will see in her story—so this process came at the perfect time to ensure that she didn't lose herself in the midst of all the changes but instead, "embraced the significance" of who she is in Christ!

As a career missionary, I have been accessed, poked, prodded, and questioned a lot—in the very best ways. I love learning about myself and my mission. Who doesn't want to be in the "sweet spot" of their gifts and offerings to God?

For most of my ministry, I have been in that very spot—by God's grace and all those assessments!

Then, at forty-three I got married, moved from my home and role of twenty plus years, and became a step-mother of four and grandmother of three—all in one glorious day. And all that change ushered in a massive identity crisis. No surprise, right? Enter the On-Purpose Person Process.

Though I knew lots about myself and what I could do well, this massive change left me flailing. How do I incorporate my gifts into partnering with a husband, caring for teenagers, and ministering in the way God has gifted me—in a new city, with few friends, and a new church?

Through the coaching process, I began to see pathways and applications for my on-purpose choices. Mary helped me remember that my purpose, Embracing Significance, begins with embracing my own significance and returning to the elements that helped me connect to my own worth in Christ—even without my old job, where I was known and competent, and without my old friends and routines.

This process ushered in new clarity for a new frontier. And I at last had a vision for how to prioritize all my new (sometimes) competing demands!

Purpose Facet

Psalm 138:3 says, "The LORD will fulfill his purpose for me." Through all life's transitions, it is comforting to know that our Father God is with you, knows each step you are taking and will take, and that you can be on-purpose in every situation—both for yourself and for others.

Are you in a life transition today? What is your current transition?

ON-PURPOSE REFLECTIONS

_____

_____

_____

$\mathcal{J}ana$

exists to serve by **Embracing Goodness**

Em-brac-ing: Welcome something eagerly or willingly; hug someone; to adopt or take up something, especially a belief or way of life. Hold close, grip, accept, welcome, adopt, support, include, involve.

Good-ness: The quality of being good, personal virtue, or kindness. Decency, honesty, integrity.

Introducing Jana

Another smart and beautiful business owner, Jana and I met through mutual friends. As she says, wearing multiple hats at the same time creates a lack of control—which I would bet most of us can relate to. Getting clarity and wearing one hat at a time is a much better look!

When I decided to take on becoming an on-purpose person, I was in my early forties, and life was starting to take on a new look. My girls were twelve and eight years old, my husband was traveling a lot, and I was feeling a large lack of control with the many hats I attempted to wear at the time.

I was and am blessed with a circle of friends that were, and remain, good tour guides into the different stages of life.

On-purpose was explained to me as a means of getting clarity and order—both of which I needed.

When I started the Tournaments, I found this was an exercise I needed to "get comfortable with," and once I did, it was completely freeing and fun. Arriving at a Core Want with the freedom of "pie in the sky" thoughts was most interesting. Each Tournament, from beginning to end, gave way to surprises and new considerations about what I *thought* was important to what was *actually* important.

For me, running the Tournaments was a part of the On-Purpose Person Process that fascinated me. Respecting the honesty that the process deserves concerning what moves forward and what doesn't kept me intrigued. I may have gone into the Tournament thinking what the outcome would be, but more times than not, I would become surprised.

However, the biggest surprise for me was my Core Want. I am a person who operates a lot from my heart. My head is always present, but the heart speaks louder in many of my decisions. What was most helpful with the On-Purpose method was that I could operate from my heart in regards to the decision, and the process gave my head the order of events to fulfill my Core Want.

On my "to do" list is to engage in this process again—and the bigger goal is to do this yearly.

PURPOSE FACET

Spending reflective time to articulate all your current wants in each of the life categories—Financial, Physical, Spiritual, Family, Vocational, Social, Mental/Intellectual, and Giving—and then running tournaments to identify the "most important" right now, brings a peace and clarity and helps us avoid the confusion and internal static that keeps you from truly knowing your purpose.

When was the last time you reflected on your own life? Will you allocate some time to really think about your wants right now?

ON-PURPOSE REFLECTIONS

_____

_____

_____

Tiffany

exists to serve by **Inspiring Significance**

In-spir-ing: Making someone feel more enthusiastic, confident, or stimulated; generating creativity or enthusiasm. Stirring, rousing, moving, exciting, stimulating.

Sig-nif-i-cance: The quality of having importance or being regarded as having great meaning. Worth, consequence, impact, importance, magnitude, substance.

Introducing Tiffany

Caution: The On-Purpose Person Process may be more than you bargained for! Tiffany was someone I worked with at Disney and one I have watched as her post-Disney career blossomed with exciting positions around the country. She began the process thinking the On-Purpose Person Process would be work-related, but her number one want surprised her (and the rest of the story is that today she is married to him!).

I think all of us are in a constant state of transition. Some transitions are perhaps more obvious than others. You have the big physical ones, like changing jobs or moving across the country. And some are subtle and more reflective, like when you are ready to make a personal leap forward in how you will hold yourself accountable.

Over my career, I have had the privilege to work with multiple organizations in executive positions, but about six months ago, my personal career batteries were at an all-time low. I had always believed my work in talent acquisition was meaningful, and I pursued it with vigor. However, for the first time in my career, I found myself completely apathetic. I had no desire to go to work, much less pursue the tasks assigned to me.

I entered the On-Purpose Person Process very open-minded, but I assumed it would tell me the three things needed to recharge my battery, and I would be back to normal. Little did I know this process would completely change my life. The process helped make the transition into thinking more deeply about a life of purpose, not status or success, and challenged me to develop new ways of evaluating my life though the Tournament process. Over the eight-week period, we discussed my life in depth to a point where I was more comfortable and able to think about how to share my thoughts with my friends and loved ones.

For many years, I have been focused on my career, with little time for a serious relationship. I traveled about 75 percent of the time and relocated three times in six years. I had always desired a meaningful relationship, but struggled to fit it into my successful and demanding work life.

One of my discoveries was how important a relationship is to me. Today, I am incredibly happy married to an amazing man. In addition, the process challenged me beyond my corporate comfort zone to consider the possibilities in the path of entrepreneurship. I launched my business coaching firm, PACE Human Capital Group, and I couldn't be happier personally and professionally.

Purpose Facet

There are always God surprises in the On-Purpose Person Process. You may think you already know yourself, but God always has new insights in store for you when your heart and mind are quiet enough to hear Him—and I can assure you, that since it is from God, the discoveries and insights are always to bless you. God has such a wonderful plan for you—more than you could ever imagine.

Do you believe that God has a specific and wonderful plan for you? Why or why not?

On-Purpose Reflections

_____

_____

_____

On-Purpose Stories

At Home

Sometimes the hardest place to be on-purpose is at home—with those we are closest to and who see us on our best (on-purpose) days and our worst (off-purpose) days. God has not made a mistake by putting us specifically in our individual family trees. He desires for us to live out our purpose with each family member.

Judy

exists to serve by **Creating Imprints**

Cre-at-ing: To bring something into existence, give rise to something, use imagination to invent things or produce works of art. Craft, form, generate, produce, fashion, design, originate, initiate, conceive, establish, start.

Im-prints: An effect that remains and is recognizable for a long time, a pattern, design, or mark that is made by pressing something down on or into something else. Impression, mark, indication.

Introducing Judy

I've known sweet Judy for many years as a dear family friend. She was a part of a church group when I facilitated the On-Purpose Person Process for a retreat of 60 women. I remember going to the Lord saying that with 60 women all at once, that He would have to do the "individual coaching" to reveal His purposes and will for these women. SO excited to share what He did!

Years ago, I attended a women's retreat where Mary facilitated the On-Purpose Person Process for about sixty women at our church. Together, we all worked through the On-Purpose materials with individual time set aside to reflect, pray, and write.

One of the sessions had an amazing outcome for me at the time. We began by reflecting on all the different categories of our lives and started to identify our Wants for each category. We would then prioritize by running Tournaments to choose what was most important to us at the time. The final round involved taking all our Top Wants for each category and running a Tournament to select the single most important want in our life at that moment!

I was really surprised that what rose to the top as the single most important want in my life at the time was to organize a family reunion. I had thought about doing a reunion "someday," but with a teenage daughter, life was too busy to add one more thing.

When we discussed our discoveries as a group, Mary emphasized the importance of moving ahead with our most important want right away. So despite my already busy life, I went to work to see if I could get this reunion organized with my very busy family across the country.

Miraculously, the reunion came together about three months later, and despite everyone's busy schedules, everyone in my family was able to come. We had been hesitant about all converging on my dad at the same time (due to his age), but decided to go for it. It was such a wonderful and blessed event, and my father was just thrilled!

No one but God knew that my father would pass not long after the reunion. I am certain that God used this process to get my attention, so that I could be focused to organize the reunion before my father was gone. I am ever grateful for this process and God's using it to push me along. I was able to say goodbye to Dad with no regrets—a true blessing!

Purpose Facet

Clarity about what's most important is the process of sorting the wheat from chaff. Since God writes desires upon our heart, when we get quiet and still, we're more apt to hear His voice directing us. Steps taken in faith today can have eternal implications we can't foresee, but God can.

What do you want your loved ones to know from you before they pass on?

On-Purpose Reflections

_____

_____

_____

Susan

exists to serve by **Sharing Blessing**

Shar-ing: To have or use something in common with other people, to allow someone to use something or have part of something, to express something to another person rather than keeping silent. Communicate, let somebody in, impart, reveal.

Bless-ing: Help believed to come from God, approval or good wishes, something to be glad or relieved about. Good thing, miracle, approval, good fortune.

Introducing Susan

Susan is one of my oldest and dearest friends—or should I restate because she will kill me—one of my friends I have known the longest! We have walked through many family and church joys and trials with her and her husband John until he passed away from Parkinson's disease. My wish for her is that she could see the amazing impact she has on others and what a blessing she is.

Although the On-Purpose Person Process was life changing for me, to be perfectly transparent, I have struggled with writing my On-Purpose story, as I feel that I am once again off-purpose.

When I went through the On-Purpose Person Process ten years ago, my life was a swirl: my father and then my sister had died suddenly, my mother had come to live with us, my only son had graduated from college and been away for five years, and I had just experienced my own battle with breast cancer. I was searching for direction, a refreshing, and a renewal—so the timing was perfect.

As I look back on my purpose work, so much of it still rings true. The process uncovered my passions of caring for people and doing for others—and my values of loyalty, honesty, encouragement, and faith.

At the time, my number one Want was to spend more time praying with my husband. My purpose statement was Sharing Blessing. I loved coming to a new understanding that instead of feeling inadequate about not working outside the home, my gift was one of availability to Share Blessing. I was excited that I could share blessing by being able to provide meals, help with airport runs, babysit, volunteer at church, and care for sick friends. My life had a new focus: that of Sharing Blessing!

Soon after going through the On-Purpose Person Process, my husband's Parkinson's disease, which had been increasingly evident over a seventeen-year period, started to accelerate. He required more and more care—to the point of a dramatic (and at times violent) decline until his death three years ago.

Over the past three years, I have been picking up the pieces as a new widow, while watching my now ninety-one-year-old mother begin her own health decline, with ongoing hospital visits and the need for much more care.

When I originally defined my purpose of Sharing Blessing, I thought of it as primarily external—sharing blessing with others outside of my home. These days, needing to be constantly at home caring for my mother, I can get very discouraged (and a bit claustrophobic). But when I can see that my purpose—for this current season—may apply on a more limited basis to Share Blessing in my own home with my own mother, I can begin to see how I can still be on-purpose.

Recently, a dear friend of mine was giving a talk at a women's gathering at our church. I wanted desperately to go and support her, but needed to stay home with my mom. I told her I would pray for her throughout the hour of her talk in my own home. I sat down and asked the Lord to be with me, and I started to write. Words came to mind, and I wrote. Scriptures came to mind, and I wrote. Before I knew it, it had been over an hour, and I felt so joyful and on-purpose! I shared the notes with my friend as a blessing and realized that I can still Share Blessings, even from my home.

When I feel cared for and safe in the Father's arms—I can again feel on-purpose. I know I need to lean on Him each and every day in order to feel blessed so that I can bless others—especially my mom.

Even though my purpose of Sharing Blessing may not always look exactly how I might define it, I am learning to Share Blessing right where I am.

Purpose Facet

Living out your purpose statement will not always be easy. I believe Jesus was the most on-purpose person who ever lived. He was clear about His purpose and lived it daily, whether He was welcomed or misunderstood—and it ultimately cost Him His life. Regardless of your circumstances, you can live out your purpose and find joy even in hardship.

When was a time you felt that you were on-purpose, but it was hard?

ON–PURPOSE REFLECTIONS

_____

_____

_____

Tami

exists to serve by **Building Confidence**

Build-ing: To form or develop something such as an enterprise or a relationship, or be formed or developed. Increase, create, encourage, foster, form, assemble.

Con-fi-dence: Self-assurance or a belief in your ability to succeed; belief or trust in somebody or something, or in the ability of somebody or something to act in a proper, trustworthy, or reliable manner; a relationship based on trust and intimacy. Self-assurance, poise, trust, support, loyalty, conviction, certainty.

Introducing Tami

Although I met and worked with Tami when she was still in her executive career at Darden, we have gotten to work much closer together with Women Doing Well. She is amazing as she continues to use her gifts and talents in her "encore career." She is proof that the word "retirement" is not in the Bible—and she continues to be on-purpose!

When I first considered the On-Purpose Person Process, my response was, "No thanks"—not because I didn't respect or value the process, but I honestly felt I pretty much knew it and had done this type of work before.

I've had my own 2-word purpose statement for years and had also thought through my vision and mission. I've been involved in a continuous spiritual growth process for many years. But with a little convincing, I soon found myself signed up for the full-blown coaching process—and I am forever grateful for that!

During the weekly sessions—and extensive "on-your-own" working time—I was able to rework my purpose statement and refine my vision and mission. All of this was very helpful. And the timing was excellent, during the fourth quarter, knowing that I could work all of this into my "plan" for the coming year.

But it was the Tournament process that was the most enlightening for me. I balked at first. It felt very "greedy" to me to be saying, "I want, I want . . . " I'm very grateful for all of the blessings that I have had in my life and for this season of abundance. But then I realized that God truly does want us to have the desires of our hearts, and I wasn't even sure what I desired!

So I began to think about what I would like in my different life areas, and I ran the Tournaments. Getting it all on a page helped me see the themes and linkages. I realized that my family was more important than I had realized and that I wanted to be more intentional about our relationships, creating special times, traveling together, and just enjoying one another.

About this time, I had the opportunity to move my mother and sister near my family—from an eight-hour drive to a two block walk! We quickly started spending time together, something that had been a luxury for our entire lives. We took field trips around central Florida; went to and watched Orlando Magic games; enjoyed plays, movies, and dinners out; shared worship; and just spent long hours reading and chatting on the porch for the next four months.

One of my "wants" had been to have a family portrait done—which became a Christmas gift to all. The true value of articulating what was important to me, and then being intentional in making it happen, blessed our family in an amazing way.

A month after the portrait was completed, my sister unexpectedly went to be with Jesus. And though you are never ready, we were so much better prepared than we might have been. We had spent so much time together that there were no regrets over "things not said," and I know that it was just what God had in mind.

Purpose Facet

Isn't it interesting when we think we know what we need to know about ourselves, and God comes to give us "new wine"? There is always more to discover about our God and who He has made you to be. May we always be willing to go deeper and see the depths of God's love for us and the marvelous gifts He has given His beloved children.

What have you learned about yourself most recently? What new aspect of God have you learned most recently?

On-Purpose Reflections

_____

_____

_____

Ann

exists to serve by **Nurturing Wholeness**

Nur-tur-ing: To give tender care and protection, helping it to grow and develop; to encourage someone or something to grow, develop, thrive, and be successful; to keep a feeling in the mind for a long time, allowing it to grow or deepen. Care for, raise, foster, cultivate, develop, cherish, support, encourage.

Whole-ness: Complete, including all parts or aspects, with nothing left out; not damaged or broken; healed or restored to health physically or psychologically. Completeness, entirety, totality, unity, fullness.

Introducing Ann

Ann and I met in an organization called J4 in Orlando whose mission is "To connect, encourage, and develop Christian women leaders to discover God's call on their lives and encourage one another to influence the world for Christ." She, Mari (you will meet her later), and I have continued to do a regular prayer and fellowship call now that she is in Tampa, Mari is in Orlando, and I am in Raleigh. She is a physician and in her current season is taking the time to care for her parents and children—God is so good in all the seasons of our lives.

As a coach myself, I find that—while it's easier to become attuned to the needs of others—this doesn't always translate into being attuned to one's own needs!

I am part of the sandwich generation. I love it. I feel blessed to be an integral part of the different layers of my family's lives. However, I found that I was being tossed to and fro with many demands. I had lost my ability to easily differentiate which were the most crucial items, and which items could just rest quietly for a while.

The long and the short of the On-Purpose process was that I was able to find what God's purpose was for me during a loud and crowded season. In running the Tournaments, my number one want was a family reunion. As a way to Nurture Wholeness, I planned and carried out (within a few short months!) the task that had previously seemed Herculean: a family reunion to celebrate my parents' upcoming sixtieth wedding anniversary. But there was an even deeper agenda: it gave me and my family a chance to begin saying goodbye to my mom, as she journeyed further along the road of Alzheimer's disease.

It was a wild and crazy reunion weekend. More than fifty of us gathered. People flew in from across the country—cousins, aunts, uncles, dear friends, and my mom's best friend from her girlhood. Stories were shared, long hugs embraced, tears were shed, songs were sung, and life was lived.

Through it all, I was able to see that God has a plan, and we have come to a mountain that can never be shaken.

I am grateful for the opportunity to have been gifted with a renewed sense of purpose.

Purpose Facet

Knowing and obeying our purpose brings deep life fulfillment—so that no matter what He may have in our life plan, we can rest in knowing that He has many seasons for us—and we can be on-purpose in every season. Jeremiah 29:11: *"For I know the plans I have for you," declares the Lord, "plans to prosper you and not to harm you, plans to give you hope and a future."*

What comes to mind when you read Jeremiah 29:11?

On-Purpose Reflections

_____

_____

_____

On-Purpose Stories

At Work

"The mass of men lead lives of quiet desperation."
—Henry David Thoreau

I like the female version of this quote: "The mass of women lead lives of aimless distraction."

Applying purpose at work enables us to see how God can use us within the daily challenges of people and career. It gives us the freedom to find ways to be more on-purpose exactly where He has placed us and use our work for His glory.

Sharon

exists to serve by **Cultivating Understanding**

Cul-ti-vat-ing: To improve or develop something, usually by study or education; to break up soil with a tool or machine, especially before sowing or planting. Develop, nurture, promote, encourage, work on, foster support, help.

Un-der-stand-ing: Ability to grasp meaning, knowledge of something, mutual comprehension. Thoughtful, considerate, comprehension, insight, awareness, appreciation, sympathy.

Introducing Sharon

I first heard about Sharon when someone told me that this amazing speaker was coming and her name was Sharon! We met again years later as a part of the Women Doing Well movement and by working alongside her for the last four years, I will tell you that next to the word gracious in the dictionary, should be Sharon's picture!

I've been a disciplined planner most of my life. Right after college, I developed a mission statement. I never could remember my mission statement, however, without pulling out my folder; but I always knew it had a teaching component in it. I would review my mission statement annually, but it never really impacted my day-to-day decisions. At times, I would feel that I was living on-purpose, but those occasions were more defined by my job assignment than by intentional daily decisions.

As a part of the Igniting Generous Joy Conferences, I originally borrowed the 2-word purpose of Connecting Meaning. I felt comfortable with it, but realized it did not feel complete. Going through the extended On-Purpose coaching process, we identified and enriched my 2-word purpose statement to Cultivating Understanding, and it fit like a glove. For me, cultivating means tending, caring for, and doing the things that promote growth. Understanding is deeper than knowledge, and I can apply understanding to train and bring clarity.

In just a few short months, it has guided me in making several key decisions. I am a partner in a three-year-old organization. As with many start-ups, each partner has worn multiple hats to get the organization off the ground. Because the organization helps women live fulfilled lives, I knew it was on-purpose for me to be part of it. However, I didn't feel on-purpose in my work! Through the use of my 2-word purpose statement, I realized that although the organization was on-purpose for me, what I was doing within the organization was not. I was spending the majority of my time doing back-end operations, because they needed to be done—rather than speaking, teaching, and writing content (my on-purpose activities). Using my purpose statement allowed me to negotiate different responsibilities with my partners. Now, both the organization and I personally win, as I contribute my best by being on-purpose.

I'm also involved in consulting ministries on leadership, strategy, and messaging. Recently a close friend invited me to partner with him on a consulting project that focused on translating technical training into creating client-oriented learning tools. Talk about being on-purpose to Cultivate

Understanding! Through this project and the clarity I've received from my purpose statement, I am focusing my consulting practice on these types of projects, so that I will more strongly serve out of my purpose.

My purpose statement has also effectively guided me in what to and not to do within my family. We've recently entered a short season wherein one of our adult children has moved in with us while transitioning to a new state. He and his wife have two young children. As we have all lived under one roof, I've seen many ways that I could become tempted to Cultivate Understanding to grow their parenting methods. Yet the word "cultivating" in my purpose statement has helped me realize that others must be willing to learn and that I can't just tell them what to do! Cultivating Understanding requires modeling as much as teaching.

Ultimately, the fulfillment of my purpose is to live out the message of Christ. I love Colossians 2:2: "My goal is that they may be encouraged in heart and united in love, so that they may have the full riches of complete understanding, in order that they may know the mystery of God, namely, Christ."

Purpose Facet

Discovering your 2-word purpose statement may take a little time and refinement. We need to walk it out, like a new pair of shoes, to see if it fits and is comfortable over time. Although your purpose statement does not change, God may continue to reveal new depths of your purpose as you dig down into who He uniquely created you to be.

Has there been a time when you felt off-purpose? What was that like?

ON-PURPOSE REFLECTIONS

_____

_____

_____

Leigh Ann

exists to serve by **Deepening Relationship**

Deep-en-ing: Get deeper, to become more intense. Intensify, extend, expand, develop.

Re-la-tion-ship: Connection, behavior or feelings toward someone, friendship. Association, connection, rapport, bond, link.

Introducing Leigh Ann

I would always see Leigh Ann's picture in the local papers for business success or community events, and she always looked so fun! Meeting her confirmed the assumption—her joy and vibrancy comes from her love of the Lord and others. Getting to know her and her purpose through this process affirms why she is so loved by God and others.

Today, I am in a very happy and grateful state—starting a new business. But it hasn't always been that way.

In 2008, I had a successful growing business with a business partner and life was going fine, so just for fun, I decided to go through the On-Purpose Person Process with two other friends. It was important that they were very close friends, because the process requires true transparency and no secrets. The environment had to be super safe.

I discovered my purpose statement to be Deepening Relationship, and my values were faith, family, honesty, integrity, and trust. It rang true to me then, but I had no idea what was in store and how it would impact me in the days ahead.

Over the next year, things deteriorated terribly with my business partner, and I was essentially kicked out of the company. It was a horrible time, and I can now see how off-purpose that situation was for me—as one who was created to Deepen Relationship rather than to *destroy relationship*.

After that partnership, my husband and I started another business together—which, as scary as it was, actually helped us deepen our relationship and made our marriage 100 percent stronger. Prior to that time, I don't think he had ever seen me struggle before, and it allowed him to step up as my protector. We now pray together every day, and I know my kids are watching and learning from us.

Today, Deepening Relationship continues to be true in my life and at home with my two children. I'm amazed that even my teenage daughter likes to hang out with me—sometimes I have to pinch myself that she still wants me to be around!

Deepening Relationship still rings true now in the third business I am starting. Knowing my purpose statement, I have been super careful about starting a new partnership. Ensuring that we are equally yoked and creating clear expectations have been part of the process so we can deepen our relationship as business partners.

God has been so very faithful to me. I just know I need to stay close to Him—and deepen my relationship with Him. I remember that in the middle of my struggles, I talked to Him every minute. I want to continue now, even when things are going well. I want to joyfully fulfill the purpose He created for me and continue to deepen my relationship with Him and others.

Purpose Facet

The depth of our purpose statement speaks to the joy of our hearts and allows us to live out the Greatest Commandment—to love God, to love our neighbor, and to love ourselves.

How would you describe your current state of how well you love God, love your neighbor, and love yourself?

On-Purpose Reflections

_____

_____

_____

Kim

exists to serve by **Liberating Clarity**

Lib-er-at-ing: To set somebody free from traditional socially imposed constraints. Release, set free, unshackle, unfetter, energizing, invigorating.

Clar-i-ty: The quality of being clearly expressed; clearness in what somebody is thinking; the quality of being clear, pure, or transparent. Clearness, simplicity, precision, transparency.

Introducing Kim

Another brilliantly smart woman in my life (surrounding yourself with brilliant people is a very good life strategy) is Kim. Thoughtful, wise, and yet transparent is how I would describe Kim. Her purpose statement applied beautifully both to her high-powered career as well as her retirement season as she cares for others and continues to seek God's clarity for her life.

I always believed, even before the On-Purpose exercises, that we each are individually endowed with attributes, talents, and desires that make for a unique person with a specific purpose in God's Kingdom. I have had a number of spiritual gift tests and personality tests, but I was still uncertain about my purpose. I felt confident that I had the spiritual gifts of teaching and prophecy. I knew I was an introvert. I knew that

I was a reader and a thinker. I saw connections and relevance among things in strategic ways.

I have to admit that I went into the On-Purpose Person Process skeptical of receiving any new insight. When we arrived at the 2-word purpose, Liberating Clarity, I felt like it was a good description—but I did not really know what to do with it. In time, I began to see how it influenced how and what I do. Those tasks that I disliked the most did not contribute to clarity and were performed without clarity. I found this frustrating. With this new knowledge about myself, I intentionally exercised more patience with others and myself in these situations.

I also see how I was on-purpose with certain opportunities in which the emphasizing and seeking clarity was a service to an organization—such as service on a non-profit board of directors. Most recently, I have seen how this desire for clarity has led to informing how I handle specific communication issues. I work closely with the president of a non-profit who uses more general terminology than I do. I find myself frequently asking, "So, what does this phrase mean to you?" I am not sure whether this is the result of my purpose or many years practicing law—or maybe both. Bringing clarity is how I bring value to discussions, organizations, and life situations.

PURPOSE FACET

Your purpose statement will confirm much of what you already know about yourself—with new insights, clarity, and the simplicity of two words. It brings an "aha" of why some experiences for you are on-purpose ("I've always done this so naturally") and why some experiences are off-purpose ("I have always hated doing that"). Living out your unique design makes sense, since it is what you were made to do!

What are the things that just come naturally for you, and people say that you do them so well?

ON–PURPOSE REFLECTIONS

Mary Ann

exists to serve by **Revealing Significance**

Re-veal-ing: Make something known, expose something, make known divine truth. Disclose, divulge, uncover, tell, bring to light, show.

Sig-nif-i-cance: The quality of having importance or being regarded as having great meaning. Worth, consequence, impact, importance, magnitude, substance.

Introducing Mary Ann

Some friends have been with you so long, you even forget how you first met. Such is the case with Mary Ann although her memory is better than mine and says she met me through my husband when we were at Disney. Mary Ann and I always have fascinating conversations mostly about the workplace and leadership behaviors—and I always cherish my time with her. She reveals significance in me!

While reading *The On-Purpose Person*, I was captivated by the thought that two words could make such a great decision-making tool. I was equally sure that my life, and especially my vocational life, was way more complex than any two words. Additionally, as a skilled trainer and facilitator, I have great trouble sitting still as a participant. The trainer rarely makes a great trainee. Yet, when God began to recraft my work life through a series of redirects—and when the opportunity arose to do the one-on-one On-Purpose coaching—I thought, "Why not?"

It is the single best thing I have ever done. It wasn't always easy or comfortable to wrestle with what I was learning and how to reconcile that with what I thought I knew about myself and my work. It wasn't easy to work the Tournaments to narrow down my Want Lists; after all, I like lists.

My 2-word purpose statement is Revealing Significance. These are the two words that actually define both my personal and vocational lives far beyond anything I could have imagined.

Even as I write this ten years later, I can tell you what most of my tournament goals were: finish a book, develop a leadership/discipleship course, grow deeper in my walk with Jesus, lose weight, build connecting relationships. And I can tell you that each one has been guided or defined and refined by Revealing Significance—even the one that remains outstanding, losing weight—which Reveals Significance about my health and life.

I use my purpose as a decision-making tool, whether in managing energy and margins or giving time and focus. At times, I have strayed from the course and have struggled and been frustrated. So I try to take the time to ask myself and God, "Is this in alignment with my purpose, Revealing Significance?" When the answer is yes, both my heart and hands labor together for a much greater impact than I ever could have imagined.

Purpose Facet

The longer you walk with your purpose statement, the more it becomes a natural part of your life and your filter for all that you will walk through in this life. Remember those new shoes I mentioned when you first get your purpose statement? Think of your favorite old "oh so comfortable" shoes or clothes that you would wear everywhere if you could. Your purpose statement becomes a very comfortable part of your life—one you couldn't imagine living without.

What is it about your favorite pair of "oh so comfortable" shoes or clothes that you love?

On-Purpose Reflections

_____

_____

_____

Kim

exists to serve by **Cultivating Prosperity**

Cul-ti-vat-ing: To improve or develop something, usually by study or education; to break up soil with a tool or machine, especially before sowing or planting. Develop, nurture, promote, encourage, work on, foster support, help.

Pros-per-i-ty: The condition of enjoying wealth, success, or good fortune. Success, riches, affluence, wealth.

Introducing Kim

One of my newest friends is from Raleigh! Kim and I met as I was working to connect with business professionals in my new city and we have become friends—both in work and with our Christian faith—a most wonderful combination. Kim is a strong and successful connector of people—and her prosperity word means a lot more than just money or success.

I didn't realize I was living off-purpose. The symptoms were there, but I didn't realize it. I was totally unaware that my life was about to spin out of control.

My life was mediocre. I had learned to settle.

And then I participated in the On-Purpose Person Process. I began to realize that I could live life instead of just survive it! I learned that it's not about the tasks I complete, but who I am made to be. I began to dream about the wants I have for my life and what my life could be like, and I uncovered hidden passions. The process uncovered a most important want that I didn't even know I had!

I am now alert to when I am being off-purpose because I feel depressed, angry, on edge, and impatient—instead of positive, enthusiastic, and content. My life now has significance. I flee from unimportant trivial matters, because they hinder me from achieving my real wants in life. My increased focus has resulted in deeper professional and personal relationships and a substantial increase in income. With whatever I am doing, I am constantly asking myself if it is keeping me on-purpose. I know becoming an on-purpose person is a lifelong process, but I am enjoying the journey!

My 2-word purpose statement is Cultivating Prosperity— cultivating means a process, taking steps to get there, and prosperity is emotional, spiritual, and financial well-being.

I have seen many of the on-purpose changes in my behavior in work-related activities. Becoming part of the solution instead of part of the problem has enhanced my credibility with management and has greatly increased my efficiency. My reactions to negativity are controlled and more objective. Now, people listen to me and take stock in some of my ideas.

One day, I was trying to present a new concept to some of my coworkers, and they were rude and interruptive, as they are typically. Since I was on-purpose, and because one of my passions is teaching, I was able to stay calm and react positively. After my presentation, those same coworkers asked me to do them a favor, which I did immediately! I also received positive affirmations from my managers; it's good to be on-purpose!

My journey to becoming an on-purpose person has already changed my life substantially, and I encourage you to start your journey!

Purpose Facet

In *Chariots of Fire*, Olympic athlete and missionary Eric Liddell is quoted as saying "I believe God made me for a purpose, but he also made me fast. And when I run, I feel His pleasure." When you discover your purpose and submit your life to His purpose for you, your outcomes will be more aligned to His plan, and you can live in joyful submission. You also will have a front row seat to watch Him bless you and others!

What is it that when you do it, you feel God's pleasure?

On-Purpose Reflections

_____

_____

_____

Amaryllis

exists to serve by **Reflecting Faith**

Re-flect-ing: Show mirror image of something or somebody, to show something, think seriously, bring credit. Mirror, imitate, replicate, reveal, suggest, show, display, think, ponder, exhibit.

Faith: Belief in, devotion to, or trust in someone or something, especially without logical proof; a strongly held set of beliefs or principles, allegiance, or loyalty to someone or something. Confidence, trust, reliance, assurance, belief, devotion, loyalty, commitment, dedication.

Introducing Amaryllis

Now you get to meet Mari (or Amaryllis as her proper name)—I mentioned her earlier in my introduction to Ann. Her on-purpose story is amazing in how God used the timing of this work to change the trajectory of her life, and I continue to receive such joy as I hear of her ongoing success for His kingdom. You just never know what God will do!

As a doctor, I started the On-Purpose Person Process after leaving a job where I thought I'd remain for a long time. This time of uncertainty opened a door to personal growth as well as unexpected opportunities. Several exercises were particularly helpful, especially setting aside time to reflect on my priorities and goals. Thinking ahead to where I wanted to be in five and ten years changed my perspective, and I began to do those things I needed to do in the short term to become the woman I envisioned.

As I refined my list of priorities, an overarching theme evolved. My number one priority was to be bold. I wanted to be like the apostle Paul. After Paul was blinded by Christ for three days, Ananias prayed over him and proclaimed, "The God of our fathers has chosen you to know his will and to see the Righteous One and to hear words from his mouth" (Acts 22:14). This is what I wanted above all things—to know God's will, to see Christ, and to hear words from His mouth.

This pursuit (and a sense of expectancy and openness to Christ's answer!) became my top priority. Everything else in my life was understood in the context of this deep desire. Grasping this as my foundation and goal, decisions became easier. Matthew 6:33 says, "But seek first his kingdom and his righteousness, and all these things will be given to you as well." This is exactly what happened.

My lifelong dream of writing resurfaced as I sought to hear Christ speak to my heart. He led me to a passage that's become my life verse as a writer. In Revelation 21:5, an angel spoke to John on the island of Patmos and said, "Write, for these words are true and faithful." I received these words as God's calling for me to use my writing to glorify Him. Specifically, I felt called to help my healthcare colleagues draw near to Christ while caring for people, letting Jesus heal and minister *to them and through them*.

I decided to cut back my patient care hours to devote two days a week to writing. I did this faithfully for over a year and, in 2012, I published my first book, *Walking with Jesus in Healthcare*. I had no idea how my life would change!

I have spent the last three years speaking to groups of doctors, nurses, and caregivers of all types about my journey as a Christian doctor. I have been able to minister to my peers during a time of crisis in healthcare when the rates of physician burnout are at an all-time high. This led to another change in focus in my career, and I now coach physicians and other healthcare professionals to help them identify burnout, rise above it, and prevent it in the future. I want to help others thrive by identifying any unused gifts, talents, and ways that people sabotage their own progress—removing obstacles and maximizing the impact of their strengths.

In 2013, I coauthored a Zondervan title, *The Ultimate Girls' Body Book.* This fun and informative book helps girls navigate the joys and challenges of puberty while seeing themselves through God's eyes. Through this book, I've been able to help girls (and their moms) to embrace their identity in Christ and believe Him rather than the lies our culture teaches about girls and women. I recently finished writing a third book, *The 3 Ys of Faith.*

The On-Purpose Person Process helped me become more intentional in every area of life, and I am healthier and feel more fulfilled as a result. As I began to pursue my top priority, other areas of my life came into greater focus as well. As I grew spiritually, I began to prioritize my well-being in every area. I started to exercise more, prioritize sleep (still my greatest challenge!), and focus on healthier behaviors and self-care. This process of walking the talk helps me be more effective and credible when I coach others to greater wholeness.

Purpose Facet

Expect transformational change when you discover your purpose. God doesn't waste anything in your life and has big plans to use you in His kingdom in a way that is custom designed for you. Matthew 19:26, "Jesus looked at them intently and said, 'Humanly speaking, it is impossible. But with God everything is possible.'"

If you could do anything and not fail, what would it be?

On-Purpose Reflections

_____

_____

_____

On-Purpose Stories

Still a Work in Progress

Identifying our unique purpose is hard work, and sometimes we need to allow our purpose reflections to simmer a while as we ponder our true purpose.

Mary Margaret

exists to serve by **Encouraging Relationship**

En-cour-ag-ing: To give somebody hope, confidence, or courage; to motivate somebody to take a course of action or continue doing something; to assist something to occur or increase. Give confidence, cheer, support, persuade, push, promote, advance.

Re-la-tion-ship: Connection, behavior or feelings toward someone, friendship. Association, connection, rapport, bond, link.

Meet Mary Margaret

When I moved to Raleigh, I had a burden for encouraging Christian businesswomen. I have experienced personally that women who have the "work gene" (like yours truly) often feel isolated on two fronts: 1) work (how do you climb the corporate ladder and maintain your Christian integrity?) and 2) church (women's ministry groups tend not to meet at times businesswomen can meet, and members of these groups often can't for the life of them understand why businesswomen actually "like" to work).

Mary Margaret was one of two women I met that shared this burden and the three of us started a Professional Christian

*Women's group in Raleigh. Isn't it amazing how God con-
nected us when Mary Margaret's (or MM as we lovingly
call her) purpose statement in progress is Encouraging
Relationship?*

When I received a copy of *The On-Purpose Person*, I read it that week! It was a quick read, and I immediately identified with the main character who had climbed the corporate ladder to a "successful" yet overly demanding position. In the beginning, he was unable to stop "feeding the monster" called work. As I read through the process he went through, at first it sounded fun and exciting, and I wanted to follow in his footsteps. Then, as I continued to read, I was confronted with a hard truth: I wanted the change in my life, but I would have to let go of my workaholic nature to get it. I laughingly refer to it as having trouble with inertia … you know … "an object in motion stays in motion until it meets another object." My winning formula has always been "work until it's done."

So there was the dilemma. Everyone who knows me has been trained by me to expect a lot of work and results. They know that I will do all that is necessary to accomplish the job—and then some! This mindset and way of living was killing me. The more I did, the more I was given. It never stopped, and I was never done "feeding the monster."

When I began the process, I had recently left my job. I was in a new place—an unknown place. I had never stepped into "nothing." I always had the next thing lined up before leaving one job to go to the next. I knew that God was calling me to "be still" for a while. But it was so uncomfortable. I was fighting within myself, and though I prayed for God to tell me what to do next, He was silent. Or more likely, He was silently working in the background in the unseen realm.

I had been in coaching before—and I had been through many

programs to help me with career paths and choices—but this was somehow different and larger in scope. I wanted to gain a NEW perspective, wanted to try a new approach, and needed to see more about myself as a whole person—not just focusing on one area. I wanted to learn something I didn't already know.

Coming up with my purpose statement was one of the hardest parts. It was difficult to choose only two words—there are so many words! I landed on Encouraging Relationship. Though I feel there are other words that would absolutely work as well, I am truly made for relationships; they are at the core of everything I do.

I have always had a heart for the underdog and the down-hearted, because I have been there myself. Encouraging others to find hope, helping them to break down big, hairy challenges into bite-sized pieces, and sharing my experiences and hope in Christ are the most rewarding and Spirit-filling joys in my life. When I'm bringing value to an area of unmet need, I am 100 percent on-purpose—no question! I feel like I am the hands and feet of Christ in a tangible way. This renews, refreshes, and invigorates me more than anything else.

The Tournaments were also challenging, and I learned a lot about the importance of choices in a new way, because they were written down on paper and right in front of me. I realized that my life up until now was all work with only a little of the "other stuff" sprinkled in. Instead of having seven top priorities in seven categories, I lived a life of a bazillion top priorities in one category—work. I had heard time and again about "work–life balance" and tried to "do" that, but I was never able to maintain any long-term balance. I had never gone through the exercise of creating a robust list of priorities in so many categories and then choosing in each category my number one (not two or three!) priority. This was eye-opening, because it was so specific, in-depth, and thought provoking. This was not a vague or random concept like "be sure to set aside time every day for family"—which I had heard a million times.

The grand finale was working on a ten-year vision. Still reeling and grieving from the heavy toll of my last work environment and trying to get my mind around "what's next"—it was beyond difficult to try and imagine farther down the road with so much up in the air. I formulated a few thoughts and filled in enough of "the blanks" to reach a point of "that's the best I can do for now." Interestingly, I felt somewhat "failed" in not having a clearer vision, but as the months passed, I reflected on how God gave me just enough to have something—not everything. It was like He was showing me how to be different and "not get it all done" in this exercise as a first step toward being a new, on-purpose person.

Fast-forward one year. Looking back on my top seven Wants in the Life Accounts, five of my seven were achieved. The other two need more work, but that is okay for now.

It is time for me to do an annual review of my priorities for the year ahead. *The On-Purpose Person* book provides easy tools to do the work. And good news: the second time around, it will be easier now that I am practiced!

Purpose Facet

On-Purpose is a process—it requires work, reflection, and even struggle. I know we would all prefer if God would just lay out our entire life plans, give us the manuals to understand every problem, and make it easy. My experience is that He delights when we are dependent on Him. As Proverbs 2:3–5 says: "Indeed, if you call out for insight and cry aloud for understanding, and if you look for it as for silver and search for it as for hidden treasure, then you will understand the fear of the Lord and find the knowledge of God." None of us has it all figured out yet. I am so grateful for His patience and helping us walk out our purpose one step at a time.

When do you feel you bring the most value to others?

ON-PURPOSE REFLECTIONS

_____

_____

_____

Jayne

exists to serve by Igniting Joy

Ig-nit-ing: To light or catch fire, arouse emotion. Stir up, kindle, awaken, provoke, incite, fire up.

Joy: Feelings of great happiness or pleasure, especially of an elevated or spiritual kind, a pleasurable aspect of something or source of happiness. Delight, happiness, pleasure, bliss, elation, thrill, delight.

Introducing Jayne

Some of the fabulous women in this book I've never even met! Jayne is one of those women—she answered the call when Kevin W. McCarthy sent out a message about this book to the women who have followed his work. I am so grateful for this larger community of women who seek to be on-purpose and am inspired by her story—I know you will be too!

My husband and I participated in a life transitions class offered at our church. We were feeling a little stuck in our lives and thought the class would help us clarify some questions and concerns we had. It was very helpful to us, and as a result of taking the class, we were invited to join an *On-Purpose Person* class that was beginning soon.

We started the class thinking that a little help would be better than none, but little did we know that it would change our lives. We each did the lessons on our own and joined in the conversations during the class. We each took away some very important life lessons, but definitely not the same ones. That was the fun part! I truly enjoyed many things about the class, but the Tournaments were an eye-opener for me. I had many Wants and had no trouble filling out the brackets, but what surprised me was that I discovered that I was lacking trust in God. I had all kinds of concerns and wants. But the constant theme that was threaded throughout the brackets was that I could accomplish many things, worry less, and find joy in each day if I only had more trust in God instead of trying to make everything happen as I wanted it on my own.

I have always been what I consider to be a strong Christian with an undying love for God, but the vision of the life I wanted was so easily clouded by my own self-doubt and worries about money and the future. I worshipped God and prayed, but I didn't really trust. As a result of this discovery, I have had my mind and heart opened to a much less turbulent outlook on the things that can so easily weigh me down and cause me to struggle and fear. I constantly remind myself that if I trust God fully, I don't have to take things on alone. I can let things go or find solutions to my concerns without having a major panic attack. I feel calmer and more equipped to deal with whatever comes my way. Do I still worry? Yes, but now I worry less and trust God more. Each day is a new beginning.

My 2-word purpose statement is Igniting Joy! I have always been a talker and a joker. I am in no way analytical or a deep thinker. The picture of Jesus laughing should have been created by me, because not only do I think He had a sense of humor, I think he probably laughs at me too. I love knowing that I have made someone's day by saying hi or having a little conversation in the grocery line. I love giving out hugs and high fives to the students and parents I work with. I love jumping out from behind the door just to make one of my kids scream. So you probably guessed it: I just like to be happy, and I want those people around me to be happy too. When I can't find that happiness, that's when I find I really need to trust God. Who knew it could be so simple, so inter-related, and so easy?

Being on-purpose is not easy. We all get caught up in life and forget the most important lessons and our purpose from time to time. My husband and I work on it together. He sends me a text almost every day after he gets on the bus to say, "Have an On-Purpose day today." I remind him as well with messages, and sometimes when we are having a conversation about how rotten things can be, I let him know that all the negativity, worry, and energy going into this problem is not allowing him or me to be on-purpose. I would recommend that each person who goes through the On-Purpose Person Process has a partner or mentor. That way, you can help each other, mentor each other, and remind each other of what is important.

I am still working on my vision board. I'm taking my time. Probably by the time I get it done, some things will already have changed for me—but I don't think it hurts to look back at where I've come from and celebrate how much more I've got to do.

Purpose Facet

I love the transparency in these stories that this process is not a "one and done"; we don't have to get it perfectly the first time. In fact, it is better that we continue to reflect, pray, and process what the Lord has revealed to us so we can continue the On-Purpose Person Process. Each and every day you can be on-purpose—which I believe brings a big smile to our Father's face as He sees his daughter doing what He created her to do.

What are some ways you can remind yourself to be and stay on-purpose every day?

ON-PURPOSE REFLECTIONS

_____

_____

_____

Wendy

exists to serve by Connecting Meaning

Con-nect-ing: To join two or more people, things, or parts; associate something or somebody with another; get along well; hit firmly. Attach, join, fix, bond, hook up, relate, associate.

Mean-ing: What something means, what something signifies, inner importance. Significance, value, consequence, worth.

Introducing Wendy

Wendy is another woman who graciously shared her story at Kevin's request. I so identify with her statement of being apprehensive about retirement. Although I know it shouldn't be, I am aware that too much of my identity is wrapped up in my work. It is encouraging to hear about other women on the journey—no matter what season we are in. She also provides such an affirming perspective that we may not instantly discover our purpose statement but it can take some time—and it is SO worth the effort!

Much of my life was structured around gaining and succeeding in a position as a school librarian, supporting my husband's and my long-term savings goals, and caring for our children and their activities, parents, church, friends, and extended family. Within that structure, I pursued fellowship in book clubs, physical exercise in different settings, and experience in life's spiritual side.

I was very apprehensive about retirement, as I understood it. On one hand, the fairly rigid structure in my workplace became constricting. On the other, I enjoyed the intellectual challenges and friendships resulting from day-to-day duties and working on larger projects involving my profession. My husband's desire for freedom from a school schedule played a large part in my decision to retire.

Retirement was a leap of faith. I hoped and expected that the first year (or years) would provide the privilege of (1) disengaging from structured work and from behaviors and beliefs that were not helpful or real, and (2) developing or creating an outlet for the skills and knowledge I had developed and enjoyed. This set the stage for beginning the On-Purpose Person Process.

Meeting with a weekly group kept me accountable and grounded in the process. I spent a lot of time in the local coffee shop, like the main character in *The On-Purpose Person* book, reading and deliberating over text, questions, and tournaments. In the first meeting, I was able to remember and share an episode that showed how troubles and peace can exist in the same moment. I find that the text and my notes in the *On-Purpose Peace* workbook are extremely helpful and provide a framework for future work.

I was afraid that I would not be able to complete the Wants Tournament, but they were completed. I was able to identify a spiritual want (learn to trust God), a physical want (know and take care of my body), an emotional or social want (strengthen family ties), and a financial want.

Identifying wants helped me to discard activities that didn't advance my most important wants and to express those wants aloud. I later learned that wants are "highly valuable and meaningful expressions of my purpose."

The wants also helped me understand that there is an Ideal On-Purpose Day, and that I need to prioritize my time. I can feel what an Ideal On-Purpose Day feels like and can get it documented. I understand that the structure of the day may change from day to day, but over time, percentages of my time can be managed to stay on-purpose.

I had hoped to develop an authentic, original, and *finalized* 2-word purpose statement by the end of the On-Purpose series of sessions. I ended by borrowing Connecting Meaning. I've been testing this purpose statement against data from a *StrengthsFinder* assessment, other writings by Kevin W. McCarthy, *Jesus Calling*, the Bible, and my own experience from what Kevin calls "high tingle." That is, I've become intentionally observant. There are many activities in the past and some in the present that spark that excitement or joy or make my heart sing and begin to clarify my purpose. Discovering Meaning or Revealing Meaning are statements that may also fit and help me to use my gifts and my time. They need daily attention and thought so that I can confidently settle on one statement that truly describes my purpose.

I continue to learn to trust God to work with me and show the way, to continue developing physical, mental, and spiritual disciplines. I can already see that I need to go through the process again to develop a stronger sense of self-leadership. I know I need to develop compassion, and I know there are false beliefs that still need exposure and discarding. One major false belief is that I had to work hard all of the time, and so must others. Another false belief is that I must always try not to inconvenience others, which is probably a trait found more frequently in women of my age and a hard one to let go.

I haven't found the perfect ending to this first year of retirement and have not yet uncovered an authentic fit for a 2-word purpose statement, but I know it's there and worth the effort. The tools, processes, vocabulary, and most of all, words of encouragement are there and in place. I'm seeking to live skillfully. I know that I can approach everything that I read and hear with skepticism, and when in terrible doubt, I can pray the Lord's Prayer. It's been a pretty good beginning.

Purpose Facet

A life of purpose is one that is in process and aware and open to what God has in store. Being in community is key to our success of being on-purpose. Many times, others see who we are more clearly than we do. I guess we can be too close to ourselves. Don't give up! I believe God honors us as we seek to know who He created us to be so we can please Him. Purpose is always in process. It's a lifelong discovery.

Who are the people God has placed in your life to come alongside of you to help, encourage, and hold you accountable?

On–Purpose Reflections

_____

_____

_____

On-Purpose Stories

Personal Clarity

"People lose their way because they lose their why."

— Michael Hyatt

Jill

exists to serve by **Liberating Truth**

Lib-er-at-ing: To set somebody free from traditional socially imposed constraints. Release, set free, unshackle, unfetter, energizing, invigorating.

Truth: Something factual, true quality, honest, faithfulness to a person or cause. Fact, accuracy, precision, exactness, honest, candor, integrity, loyalty, devotion, uprightness.

Introducing Jill

So excited for you to meet my powerhouse friend Jill—consultant, speaker, coach, radio talk show and TV host, author, and all-around dynamic person! Our initial meeting was such a God thing, and we've stayed in touch as she continues to drive and thrive and change the world. Her purpose statement has become her brand! I told you she was dynamic!

It was as if my life were *A Tale of Two Cities*. I felt as if *"It (my life) was the best of times, it was the worst of times, it was the age of wisdom, it was the age of foolishness ..."*

I was seemingly at a height in my career, responsible for leading some of the best and most rewarding projects of my human resources journey. It was all very challenging and impactful, and I was receiving recognition for first-ever program launches from my employer. Yet I could not shake the nagging feeling that I was off-target in pursuing what I was divinely created to achieve in my life.

I had no work colleagues who I believed would be objective, private, spiritual, or patient enough to listen to my concerns. Even among my prayer partners, I was unable to effectively express why I was feeling "off-kilter." Wasn't I living the blessed life of material reward, vacation, travel, and service to my community and church? Nonetheless, from time to time, I succumbed to my "whining" prayer requests, feeling all-too-uneasy each time I verbalized, "There's just something not quite right going on in my life. I don't know what it is, but I'm off target."

And while I'm certain my prayer partners loved me dearly, comments such as, "What do you have to complain about?" or "There's always someone worse off than you," caused me to retreat and focus on interceding for others who had bigger issues than I did.

Then one day, there was a particular workplace incident that made me question, "What am I doing here?" So I asked the Lord, "God, please send me someone who understands corporate work life and is a believer." I felt like I received an immediate response. That very week as I opened my email from home, I received information about the On-Purpose Person Program.

At our very first meeting, Mary asked a question that I could not answer: "What were you divinely created to do?" I needed to be able to answer the question by completing the statement, "I was divinely created by God to serve others by [BLANK] [BLANK]," and fill in the two blanks. So I thought, "Wasn't I doing what I was supposed to be doing?" It would certainly take more than two words to describe what I was created to do. However, I thought since I was questioning my current position in life, it was clear I needed to take the journey of discovering my God-ordained life purpose.

Through the eight-week coaching process, my purpose was revealed. Through the facilitated coursework, by the end of the program, I was able to complete the sentence, "I was divinely created by God to serve others by Liberating Truth." Friends and family have often confirmed that I always have to "get to the bottom of everything" or "peel back the onion" of every matter. Yes, Liberating Truth is who I am and what I do.

Over the years, I have heard many sermons and lectures about the significance in knowing one's purpose. But the On-Purpose Person Program clarified, defined, and revealed my purpose—and that it was unique from that of any other person. Not to be confused with talents and spiritual gifts, I came to know my purpose as my life anchor. Regardless of my age, circumstance, or status, my purpose will never change—and has to be fulfilled. Only through this facilitated birthing process did I discover why my soul was not at peace when everything externally appeared to be right or good. I found deep within that everything was not A-okay, because I was off-purpose!

The On-Purpose Person Program provided the components of explaining and identifying my mission, vision, values, and goals and aided me in becoming clearly focused on where to invest time and energy at that specific point in life. In all the busyness of my life at that time, I realized I needed to spend more time and focus on my teenage daughter. Everything else was secondary.

Today, Liberating Truth is the very fiber of my being, and no longer tucked away. Since my discovery nearly eight years ago, my purpose statement has been at the forefront of my ministry work. In my own company, it's my brand; I serve others by Liberating Truth! I now have radio and TV programs by the same name, which teach and reveal the Word of God—along with a Liberating Truth logo, business cards, and letterhead.

Does life require that we go this far with our purpose statements? No, but why wouldn't we? For me, celebrating God and who He's called me to be with confidence and certainty is freeing.

Purpose Facet

On-purpose marks a distinct moment of clarity. Moving forward, life will never be the same. It is like the key that unlocks your future in the Lord and how He can use you in new and powerful ways for His glory. If you feel any "holy discontent" in your life right now, perhaps the Holy Spirit is creating this discomfort to draw you unto Himself and all He has planned for you since the beginning of time.

Is there any "holy discontent" in your life right now—where you feel the Holy Spirit is trying to move you to a new place? Describe below.

On-Purpose Reflections

_____

_____

_____

Judy

exists to serve by **Redeeming Significance**

Re-deem-ing: Make something acceptable, to do something that changes a negative opinion to a positive one, to fulfill a pledge or promise. Release, liberate, free, rescue, deliver, save.

Sig-nif-i-cance: The quality of having importance or being regarded as having great meaning. Worth, consequence, impact, importance, magnitude, substance.

Introducing Judy

Another powerhouse in a gentle way is my friend Judy. She has a powerful perspective and insight of how our purpose has been impacted by the generations before us. Her compelling story and special purpose serves her perfectly as she advises people on their financial legacy. God has such interesting roles for His daughters to play—each as unique as we are!

My On-Purpose journey began in 2007 as I was starting my fifth decade. By this age, I was certain of my spiritual gifts. Still, I was restless for more. I wanted to make sure I was on-purpose. People may say I was a late bloomer, which would be true.

During our coaching, I was asked to consider the purpose

statement of Redeeming Significance. I walked away smiling; one of my words involved faith, and I thought that fit. But I wondered at first what Redeeming Significance meant. Since that day, the Lord has shown me dozens of ways He wants to Redeem Significance in my life and the lives of others. Here is one of those stories.

Have you heard of Gen 4? Not Genesis 4, but Generation 4. If you pick up any business periodical, eventually you will see an article on Gen 2 and Gen 3. The etymology comes from the concept of a patriarch or matriarch who creates wealth and wants to transfer it to the second and third generation by creating a multigenerational legacy. But what is Gen 4, and how do generational legacies apply to the covenant of God?

When I think about generational legacies, I think about two families: Abraham (Gen 1), Isaac (Gen 2), Jacob (Gen 3), and Joseph (Gen 4)—and I think about my Great-Grandmother Hubbard.

In looking at the generations of the patriarch Abraham—Isaac and Jacob—we see the wealth was passed down from Abraham through Isaac to Jacob, but so was the dysfunction and sin. Abraham had a tendency to lie, Isaac showed favoritism, Jacob was deceptive, and Joseph could be braggadocious. He loved his new coat. The examples of the biblical patriarchs may indicate that while wealth can be inherited, wisdom may not.

This reminds me of the story of my great-grandma and the subsequent impact on future generations. My great-grandma was a true matriarch. Around the time that Oklahoma was becoming a state, she began building her wealth, one piece of property at a time. Known for her keen business acumen, after accumulating vast land holdings, she eventually also came to own the general store and the bank. Even on the day of her death at age eighty-two, she was out measuring land to buy. Unfortunately, with the passing of my great-grandma, soon came the demise of her wealth.

Great-grandma's estate was large enough to last many generations. But just ten years later, all her money was gone! How could this alarming loss happen so quickly? Perhaps it was the lack of the transfer of wisdom.

The pain for the family did not just come from the loss of the money, but the circumstances and personal failures that accompanied it. The horror stories about my dad (Gen 3) losing his inheritance came with tremendous shame and embarrassment. We lived in a small rural town, and his dealings were known by most. As each asset was sold, my dignity was chipped away. The conversations over the worry of money were a constant theme in our home. As a little girl, this was too much for me to emotionally handle.

From the early age of five, I lived in constant fear. I went to bed worrying if there would be enough money to provide food and shelter, and whether I would be safe at night. It took me hours to fall asleep, lying awake worrying. Every day and every night for the next twenty-seven years, I was consumed with fear of the lack of money. To top it off, I had no hope—no hope for getting out of this miserable state. I wondered how I would ever break this vicious cycle.

A Catalyst for the Change

When I was thirty-two years old, I moved to Orlando with the love of my life. I was sure Florida would be the land flowing with milk and honey. Instead, I found Egypt. Just like Joseph, it seemed I was in prison—except I had two prisons. I was still in the prison of fear about lack of money, and now a second prison—a dysfunctional relationship. My world was turned upside down. Through one painful act of my beloved, my heart was completely broken. The emotional suffering was so severe I thought I would die, and I wanted to die for many, many years. I was in a fetal position more than once as I came in touch with the pain, only to camouflage it with a smile.

I was sure the pain was going to kill me, but God had another idea. He wanted to redeem me. I did not know it then, but I understand now that God was orchestrating a beautiful symphony—a symphony better than the Royal Concertgebouw Orchestra of Amsterdam or the Vienna Philharmonic. I had yet to discover that my worst pain was going to be my GREATEST VICTORY, and that was where the real God journey began.

It was out of my extreme suffering that the layers and layers of my wounded heart had a chance to be healed. It was the beginning of my painful refining years, the removing of the dross. I began to really search for God's truth. James 1:2–4 became my mantra: "Consider it all a joy, my brothers and sisters, whenever you face various trials, because you know that the testing of your faith produces perseverance. Let perseverance have its perfect and complete gift, that you are not lacking anything." I also held onto Ephesians 6:12: "For our warfare is not against flesh and blood, but against principalities and places of darkness." I realized that the only way I could wage war was with the sword, the Word of God.

Soon I began to discern Satan's lies and deception. Bible Study Fellowship was a lifeline for me, and Howard Dayton's biblical study on money began to set me free from the fear of lack of money. I memorized every verse of Howard's study. So how does this apply to God's generational covenant for me?

A Generation Redeemed

I was the Gen 4 in my family line from my great-grandma. Joel 2:25 became especially meaningful to me: "I will redeem the years the locusts have eaten." I prayed that Scripture for twenty years, never imagining what would become of that prayer. Yet I prayed faithfully and held no expectations. Then one day—one appointed day—God said to me, "Judy, I want to redeem all the years the locusts have eaten in your life, including what your great-grandma left."

I thought, "What Lord, did I hear you correctly?"

He said it again, "Judy, I want to redeem the years the locusts have eaten in your life for you, your sister Cynthia, and for other families." I had to hear it five or six more times before I could believe it. But it was the Lord's covenant to me. I learned that God's plan was to bless others through my generation.

I was reminded of another covenant, the Abrahamic Covenant, that says the families of the world would be blessed through the physical line of Abraham. Genesis 12:3 states, "I will bless those who bless you, and him who dishonors you I will curse, and in you all the families of the earth shall be blessed." Genesis 22:18 adds, "... and in your offspring shall all the nations of the earth be blessed, because you have obeyed my voice." God's covenant to me was about generational redemption.

Covenants are generational. When we humble ourselves and pray, so many things can be redeemed. Through all these years of pain, God prepared me for a career of helping to redeem generational wealth and investing wisely in future generations—as a financial advisor.

Praise God for His miraculous word and wisdom! He uses all our years for His glory.

Purpose Facet

Won't it be fun to get to heaven and finally understand how God has used your generational history to bring about His unique design for you? In your family line, each person has had impact on your life whether we knew them or not. God knew exactly who you were, when you would be born, and the impact you could have during your own time on this earth. May each of us live out our lives with true and passionate purpose to impact future generations. Our purpose redeems the past AND the future.

What are some things you know about your family generations before you and how they have impacted your life?

On-Purpose Reflections

_____

_____

_____

Tomeka

exists to serve by **Setting Free**

Set-ting: To put somebody or something into a particular condition, to cause something or somebody to begin doing something, or begin to do something, to focus your mind on a goal or task, to consider something as having a particular value. Place, position, establish, agree.

Free: Not, or no longer physically bound or restrained, e.g. as a prisoner or in slavery; not restricted in rights; not regulated; open and honest. Liberated, unbound, limitless, released, uninhibited, open.

Introducing Tomeka

So many of us start our purpose journeys in a messy place. We are juggling many balls and feeling frustrated about our current situation but don't know how to make sense of it or how to move forward. The On-Purpose Person Process provides the insights to unlock the life we desire but it is a process—we have to walk it out each and every day. Tomeka is a wonderful example of taking this work one day at a time.

My life before the On-Purpose Person Process was blurry. Life throws many obstacles your way. Obstacles can be with a job, family, finances—or with one's self; and not having a clear vision or purpose makes life challenges hard to bear. I did not know what the process had in store for me, but I did know I was willing to try for the sake of knowing that there had to be more.

I always felt that there was something I was missing. My brain is very methodical, so there had to be some method to the madness. I felt as though one day, some life-changing decision would force me to a fork in the road. I hoped this process would help empower me with the right change management approach, so that I would not have to remain at the same fork.

My past personal life had been what I call challenged. I always thought because I wasn't born with a silver spoon in my mouth and not under the best circumstances, that I never had the proper guidance to make better choices. I was taught to stumble and learn from the falls. However, in many cases, I continued to trip or stumble on my rocky road.

I can easily admit to this, because I am consciously aware that I had always put so much of myself out there that I never had anything left in return for myself. I always wondered why I could not get it together, or why I ended up in these precarious situations. I didn't know any better, and I didn't have a fallback plan.

The irony is this: as a project manager professional with more than sixteen years' experience, I possess high critical skills in managing many complex, multi-million dollar technology projects with large global teams. However, I could not seem to manage my own personal life. I was so caught up in the corporate dream of getting to the top. There were conflicts I had internalized because there was a constant uneasiness in achieving my career goals while trying to maintain work–life balance.

As time moved on, I recognized that my life had become complicated with so many balls up in the air, and I was constantly struggling to keep them all from crashing down. Through the years—while maintaining a career—I had gone through a divorce, experienced failed relationship after failed relationship, and was left to raise and support my two loving kids and an aging mother. Not to mention, I served as a sounding and financial board for all my extended family members. I had no other choice but to look deeper and try to discover my purpose.

After completing my On-Purpose Person Process, my 2-word purpose statement is Setting Free! Now that I understand this, my purpose statement is in the forefront of my everyday decision making process. After running the Tournaments, I now understand what is most important for me in each of my Life Accounts.

Before this process, my mind was caught up in a jungle of thoughts—inter-tangled, all jumbled up together— which clouded my judgments and decisions. My vision was constantly blurry, and my goals were neither clear nor achievable. Now, after knowing my Core Wants and understanding my vision and goals, I have the stepping stones to Setting Free.

I know it will be a constant journey—such as baby steps leading to toddler steps, toddler steps leading to adolescent steps, and adolescent steps leading to adult steps—but there is constant progression and wisdom. Staying focused, on target, and on-purpose is the key.

This process was a powerful spiritual awakening for me. To grow with the plan that God has designed for me is powerful. Being able to recognize when I am deviating from the plan and knowing when to fall back or revise when necessary is powerful. Most importantly, the On-Purpose Person Process feels right!

Purpose Facet

The truth is that no one is on-purpose 100 percent of the time. The beauty of knowing your purpose is that we can identify quickly when we are off-purpose, and can run (not walk) back to our Father's arms as our designer and ask Him to be on-purpose in our lives. It is a journey, and each day we can once again choose to live as on-purpose daughters of the King. The goal is to be a little more on-purpose every day.

What percent of your time (out of 100 percent) would you say you are currently living on-purpose? Why?

On-Purpose Reflections

_____

_____

_____

JoAnne

exists to serve by **Connecting Joy**

Con-nect-ing: To join two or more people, things, or parts; associate something or somebody with another; get along well. Attach, join, fix, bond, hook up, relate, associate.

Joy: Feelings of great happiness or pleasure, especially of an elevated or spiritual kind; a pleasurable aspect of something or source of happiness. Delight, pleasure, bliss, elation, thrill.

Introducing JoAnne

Love this next story from another one of Kevin's fans. Such great insights, especially about woodpeckers—no wonder we feel attacked when our lives are hollow! I would say to this sister in Christ: "Preach it, Sister!"

Iwas participating on a conference call with one of my favorite mentors, Kevin W. McCarthy. In the course of his presentation, he made the statement that "woodpeckers only knock on hollow trees." The truth is, woodpeckers fly around knocking on many trees, and they keep on knocking until they find the hollow ones. They can tell by the sound that the tree is hollow, and they know by the hollow sound that the tree is dying and decaying—and is full of insects on which they will feast. Once the woodpecker determines which trees are solid and which are hollow, it abandons the ones with the solid core and continues to peck with a vengeance at the hollow trees. Interesting, hmmmm...

It occurred to me that the woodpecker's knock could be used to describe the challenges that each of us face from time to time on our journeys of life. These challenges and crises show up in many forms, such as the loss of someone close to us through illness, death, or broken relationships. People lose their jobs, the economy takes a downturn, there are accidents, and we make mistakes. The list is endless. Through these tough times, we do have a choice: either give up or learn how to work out a successful outcome. We will come through victoriously if we have a solid core of values and inner strength. Very likely, we will have learned some valuable life lessons that will equip us to deal more adeptly with the next "knock of life." Without this solid core of our being, the suffering and struggle may go on much longer. We may never learn the lesson, leaving us even more vulnerable when the next "knock of the woodpecker" arrives. I believe it is essential to consciously work on strengthening one's core, so it will be solid, strong, resilient, and vibrantly alive.

As humans, we are made up of body, mind, and spirit. To stay strong and healthy, we need to nurture all three areas and build up muscle and strength. Care for the body involves making good nutritional choices to fuel this vehicle that drives us through life. We need to exercise. We need sufficient sleep and relaxation to stay in top form.

At one point, I recall being so absorbed in my work as a realtor that I had a standing appointment with my mechanic for regular maintenance for my vehicle. I would tell him, "Garry, do whatever you need to make sure that my car runs well and that I won't be left stranded in between appointments. After all, time is money." One day, I realized that I had not had a physical checkup with my doctor on my body in more than three years. How foolish to neglect my personal vehicle of life, which is not replaceable, while tending so diligently to my car, which was easily replaceable.

Our mind also needs exercise through the stimulation of learning, studying, and growing. It needs to be fed with strong positive messages to build mental muscles. Perhaps subscribe online to daily positive messages. Read good books. Choose positive friends. Our spirit must be nurtured daily through taking time for solitude, meditation, or some form of prayer. When we quiet the spirit, we open ourselves to the guidance and direction that comes our way. I must mention here that it is necessary to forgive and let go of resentment to keep the spirit healthy.

Sometimes we can lose ourselves along the way. Tough life experiences can be devastating, and we find ourselves feeling lost and wondering what life is really all about.

This is where I was at the end of the year 2000! In 2001, I had an experience which produced a lasting effect that has been the catalyst for change in my life. This occurred during a very busy time with work and family. We were in the process of moving from our large family home. Two of our three sons were moving on to other cities, and our other son was engaged and planning to marry. I was very exhausted from juggling my busy work as a realtor and caring for our family— and my self-care was almost nonexistent. I felt like life was passing so quickly and that I was missing out on many of the really important things in my life. Outwardly, I looked very successful, but inside, I felt empty and on a treadmill— with little joy and plenty of stress. Maybe "the empty nest syndrome" had already struck. Looking and searching, not even sure what I was looking for, I picked up the book *The On-Purpose Person*, subtitled *Making Your Life Make Sense*. The subtitle really caught my attention.

I read these words on the back cover: "Is your life filled, yet unfulfilled? Do you feel pulled in a number of different directions? Does your schedule seem totally out of control? Have you been trying to live up to everyone else's expectations, while your own plans and dreams go unfulfilled?" I could relate to almost every question there.

So I sat down and read it. In the back of the book, I read the words, "Would you like to become an on-purpose guide and help others become on-purpose?"

I said sarcastically to myself, "I sure would, if I only had a clue where I was going." I made a phone call to the number in the back of the book. The lovely lady on the line said, "Oh, perhaps you would like to participate in the upcoming two-day workshop/retreat that the author Kevin W. McCarthy is conducting at the end of the month in Orlando, Florida." *I knew I had to be there.*

Several issues had to be rearranged to make it possible. My husband and I live in Windsor, Ontario, Canada, and were already booked to fly from Detroit to a conference being held Friday through Sunday in Fort Worth, Texas. I needed to check in for Kevin's program on Sunday night to start on Monday morning. I set about to alter our flight schedules. The nice young man at United Airlines said it would be an extra $800 each to add that leg onto our trip. I said to him, "But you don't understand. I need to be there, and that fare is way too costly for me." I wrote down his name, asked him to work on it, and said I would call back the next day. Well, Divine Providence moved too. When I called back, the additional fee was $200. This was accomplished by flying back to Washington and on to Orlando. I attended the two-day program of looking at my life from a different perspective—through new lenses, so to speak.

My time there impacted my soul deeply, and I have never

been the same. I got to the core of who I am as a person and defined my 2-word, concise, yet all-encompassing purpose statement—Connecting Joy. I could see that my purpose had been there since my youth; it was there then and would remain with me into the future. It provided me with a deep feeling of significance, gave new meaning to my work, and filled my life with a sense of Divine Order. It left me with a sense of awe that God had created me "uniquely."

Making my lists for the various Life Accounts was very difficult. I realized that I had stopped asking myself what I *really* wanted and usually settled for whatever I thought was reachable—and whatever wouldn't rock anyone else's life. I had become used to doing "what needed to be done" to earn a living after our previous business had failed. I was in survival mode. It took a great deal of courage even to allow myself to write down my heart's desires on those sheets. I could not see how they could ever happen!

I have reviewed the On-Purpose Person Process frequently, at least annually, for the last fourteen years. I have received focus, clarity, and the courage to eventually let go of commitments and involvements that were not well aligned with my purpose. My priorities have gradually changed; this process has been the catalyst for many changes since then. I believe I have a much higher quality of life—in many areas of my life—because of my experience applying the On-Purpose Person Process. I learned that it is not about prioritizing my schedule. It's about defining my priorities and then scheduling my highest priorities into my day. My business has blossomed, my relationship with myself and others has become richer, and my appreciation of the gifts in my life has grown. The level of joy in my life amazes me. The satisfaction of connecting others to the joy in their lives is so rewarding. I have revisited my Purpose, Vision, Mission, and Values Statements numerous times, and I now use them to remind myself of who I want to be in this life.

I shared this process with a small group of friends, and beautiful things happened in their lives. Sharing this with others has helped me to strive for progress. It's been fourteen years since that on-purpose experience. Many of my deepest dreams have been fulfilled over this time: the writing and publishing of my first book, speaking to groups, and facilitating this life-giving On-Purpose Program for others. I am more Spirit led now and make my choices guided by my purpose: Connecting Joy. I continue to stay in touch with Kevin and share his invaluable program. I believe this process has really helped me to become more solid in the core of my being as "protection from the woodpecker's knock."

I urge you to search and clearly find your authenticity and purpose—not only for your own growth and development, but so you can make a difference in the lives of those around you. Only *you* can deliver the gifts that you have been given. Remember: we really do find more of ourselves when we are in the service of others. Finding, defining, and living our purpose creates authentic success for ourselves.

Purpose Facet

If your life is feeling hollow—and you find yourself needing to constantly "shoo away" the doubts, uncertainty, shaming voices, and feelings of despair—it may be time to allow yourself to be quiet and thoughtful about God's purpose for you. A full and on-purpose life is sure to keep all the pesky woodpeckers away!

Where do you feel most vulnerable to Satan's attacks as pesky woodpeckers?

ON-PURPOSE REFLECTIONS

_____

_____

_____

Janet

exists to serve by **Awakening Worth**

A-wa-ken-ing: To wake up from sleep or a similar state; just beginning or growing; a sudden recognition or realization of something; a revival or renewal of interest in something, especially religion. Development, beginning, start, stirring, arousing, initiation.

Worth: Important, large, or good enough to justify something; the goodness, usefulness, or importance of somebody. Value, meaning, appeal, significance.

Introducing Janet

In word association, I would use "charismatic" to describe my next friend Janet. Kevin and I had the pleasure of working with her in a number of businesses and I would never have guessed about her low self-worth—but don't we all hide our less desirable parts pretty well? I am grateful that God has revealed her true purpose so that she can bless the socks off those she meets!

Several years ago, a dear friend handed me a book titled *The On-Purpose Person*, by Kevin W. McCarthy. This message and writing my 2-word purpose statement of Awakening Worth changed my life and continues to shape me in decision making, performance, and being true to my purpose and values.

I have struggled with low self-worth for most of my adult life. Although I am successful and have achieved most of the goals I have set for myself throughout my life, my poor self-worth has kept me hostage to guilt, approval seeking, and people pleasing. When my husband asked me what I wanted for my fiftieth birthday, I told him I wanted to attend a seminar in Orlando titled *Power Up On-Purpose*, led by the author of the book I had just read.

The seminar promised that at the conclusion of the weekend, each participant would leave the event with a personal purpose articulated in two words and more. That was exactly what I wanted. So I purchased my airline ticket, got on a plane, and flew three thousand miles from my home in Southern California to Orlando, Florida.

My purpose statement has been life changing for me. Without question, the culminating blessing of defining my personal purpose is becoming the author of my own book, *Going to the Well—A Journey to Awakening Worth*.

Discovering my purpose allowed me to focus on what matters most to me by aligning my choices with my purpose, i.e. being on-purpose. Until I gave myself permission to write and decided I truly had something of value to say, I continued to make excuses for why the book wasn't completed. People pleasing, approval seeking, and making other people's expectations of me more important than my dreams and purpose "excused" me from writing. Eventually, the worth of being myself exceeds the pain and cost of being off-purpose. And so I wrote my book, and it was released in 2014. It was only when my worth was awakened that I could more fully awaken the worth of others.

Today I celebrate who I am, why I exist, and who I serve. I have discovered my place and am joyful in it. Candidly, day to day, my circumstances and life events still cause me to question my self-worth and contribution. Being on-purpose isn't always easy, but turning on my light switch always brightens my spirit even in the midst of the darkest of times.

Thanks to the On-Purpose Approach, I am inspired to live every day Awakening Worth. And now through my life and work—but especially through my book—I get to help other women do the same.

PURPOSE FACET

Finding your purpose brings such freedom and joy. You no longer have to compare yourself to anyone else. You finally know your own uniqueness and don't need to be like anyone else! Those with purpose can live a life that is certain of God's unique design and allow others to do the same.

When do you most compare yourself to others? What would God say to you?

ON-PURPOSE REFLECTIONS

_____

_____

_____

Debra

exists to serve by **Restoring Worth**

Re-stor-ing: Give something back, return something to previous condition, energize somebody, to give somebody new vigor or strength, put something back. Reinstate, repair, bring back, return, rebuild.

Worth: Important, large, or good enough to justify something, the goodness, usefulness or importance of somebody. Value, meaning, appeal, significance.

Introducing Debra

We have always heard the saying, "God doesn't give us more than we can handle." And our response often is "Oh really, I sure don't see it like you do!" My friend Debra has had some life challenges but her true worth has been restored through Christ and she restores worth in others. She is a precious daughter in Christ and I hope she feels this each and every day.

My on-purpose friend, Jill, referred me to the On-Purpose Person Process. At the time, I was unemployed, confused, severely depressed, and just going in circles in my life. I felt like I was following all the rules and doing everything I knew to make my life work, but nothing seemed to go right for me.

In the midst of my chaos, I met Mary. She looked at my resume and said she saw so much potential for me. Inside my head, I was saying, "Then why don't I have a job? Why don't I have a career?" I could hear the little whiny voice in my head going, "Woe is me, nothing good ever happens to me, what happened to my life, nobody cares, everybody is successful but me." I was the "Queen of 'Pity Parties.'" Having a "pity party" is an art, and I had mastered it.

I decided to go through the On-Purpose Person Process, and I truly enjoyed it. I chose to go through the process, because I admired my friend Jill's faith and "never say die" attitude. I felt safe with the process and with Mary; she did not judge me but encouraged me and wouldn't let me give up on the process once I started. She would let me vent but never agreed with anything negative I said about myself or my life. I wanted to say, "Don't you see, I am just a loser." Mary didn't see a loser in me; she saw someone who needed coaching, encouraging, and direction in that time of my life.

I discovered a lot about myself during the On-Purpose Person Process. I loved the Tournaments. They made me feel hope—not false hope, but genuine hope. I remember thinking, "Maybe my life really can get better, maybe it is not too late to be what I want to be, maybe my life isn't over, and maybe I am not a loser, just a late bloomer."

The process put a spark inside of me that I still cherish today. I have not accomplished all of my goals that I set for myself during my first On-Purpose work, but I have not given up on my dreams, my goals, my aspirations, and my life.

One of the highlights of the process was coming up with my 2-word purpose statement. When I finally agreed on my purpose statement, it scared me at first. I exist to serve by Restoring Worth. I was broken and felt worthless, so I couldn't see how this statement could honestly describe me.

Over the last few years, I have come to realize that your test becomes your testimony. Your pain becomes your ministry to others. Even though I felt broken and worthless, I still enjoyed helping and serving others. In my profession today, the joy I get from Restoring Worth in my students is priceless.

Growing in life is a process, not a destination. Nothing has changed for me overnight. I still have my moments, but I have learned how to snap myself back to my on-purpose reality really quickly. Life is NOW! Embrace the moment!!

All the time I was going through my On-Purpose Person Process, I knew a part of me wanted to be an On-Purpose coach someday; it's a goal that I know will come to pass one day. I want to be able to reach out and touch people and let them know *they are not alone and they are not the only ones on this planet going through a lonely time.* Never give up; lonely times are temporary. Life is good and waiting to dance with you! Be on-purpose!

Purpose Facet

The revelations of discovery in an on-purpose life are deep and lasting. When you experience something that is life changing (such as your relationship with the Lord), there is an urgency, as you want so desperately to share it with the world. I love how Debra says: "Growing in life is a process, not a destination. Nothing has changed for me overnight. I still have my moments, but I have learned how to snap myself back to my on-purpose reality really quickly. Life is NOW! *Embrace* the moment!!"

What is it that you need to embrace in this moment today?

ON-PURPOSE REFLECTIONS

_____

_____

_____

Eileen

exists to serve by **Setting Free**

Set-ting: To put somebody or something into a particular condition, to cause something or somebody to begin doing something, or begin to do something; to focus your mind on a goal or task, to consider something as having a particular value. Place, position, establish, agree.

Free: Not, or no longer, physically bound or restrained, e.g. as a prisoner or in slavery; not restricted in rights, not regulated, open and honest. Liberated, unbound, limitless, released, uninhibited, open, emancipated.

Introducing Eileen

Some of us grew up in Christian homes and some of us did not. There's no magic formula for any of us—we each need to discover who God made us to be. And this retirement season has come up several times. It's valuable to be aware that it can be a real shock to our system but also know that we can be prepared to be on-purpose in every season!

Growing up in a Christian family, religion and church attendance were a big part of my everyday life. I knew God loved me, and He would always be with me. As an adult, my life pretty much modeled that of my growing up years. We attended church, our kids attended Sunday school, and life was good.

I worked outside the home for thirty-plus years, mostly full time. Then one day, I found myself retired! The day should have been the most relaxing and stress-free day of my entire life. I had planned it; I knew the date; and I was looking forward to it. The day came, and I felt utterly lost! What would I do with the next eight hours? Or, what would I do with all day, every day?

I had no direction. I had allowed my outside work to define me, and that was over. You might say I was overwhelmed, and I needed to get to the core of who I was: my purpose! When I heard my church was offering a study session on *The On-Purpose Person: Making Your Life Make Sense,* I knew I had to sign up!

The class was designed to help us "declutter" our lives, so to speak, and get to know what was truly important to us. We wrote down our Wants Lists in different life categories. Once I started to write them down, more and more Wants came to me. Then, we ran our Tournaments—taking our Wants Lists and choosing the one which was most important to us. This was not easy, but the surprising thing was that when I identified my Core Want, I had also clarified all my smaller wants—such as personal happiness, being grateful and thankful for the things I had, spending more time with my family, helping others, and staying healthy.

The book talks about "redeeming time," which clearly spoke to me in retirement! There is still time to "live into God's purpose." The "spent" years are now redeemed as "invested" years. Running the Tournaments helped me to see that. Removing the clutter in my life helps me become the person God intended for me to be: to become aligned, and to be set free!

Purpose Facet

Our true identity is in our purpose—not in what we do or who we care for. We have purpose after the kids go away to college or the work life ends. God is a big God with big plans for our lives from birth to the grave. Society may try to define us by what we do, or how much we make, or where we live, but God defines us by who He made us to be. May we each discover our purpose and walk it out every day of our lives. No matter what season we are in, we can be wonderfully on-purpose.

What could decluttering your life look like for you?

On-Purpose Reflections

_____

_____

_____

Julie

exists to serve by **Discovering Beauty**

Dis-cov-er-ing: To find out information that was not previously known, to realize for the first time that you enjoy or have a talent for something; recognizes someone's potential for success. Find out, learn, determine, come across, uncover, locate, detect, encounter.

Beau-ty: Something very good, attractive, or impressive of its kind; an attractive, useful, or satisfying feature; pleasing and impressive qualities of something. Loveliness, splendor, magnificence, attraction, exquisiteness.

Introducing Julie

Another precious friendship from God has been Julie. We met when she was working for Kevin and have kept in touch over the last 15 years (if you ever need the most phenomenal proofreader you have ever seen, you need Julie). Love how she lives her purpose statement in life and work and I know you too will discover beauty as you read Julie's story.

My On-Purpose journey is different from many others. I was in a transition time in life and looking for work after leaving a toxic work environment. I found a job posting and replied to it. It turned out to be the administrative assistant to Kevin W. McCarthy. Soon after I started working there, an On-Purpose Person one-day workshop was being held. I was invited to come along to experience it so that I could be more aware of the information and services we offered.

When the exercise of coming up with the 2-word purpose statement started, I became a bit stuck. I focused on objects of "worth" and "value," which were close but not quite there. At the time, I settled onto Nurturing Wholeness as my purpose statement. While I didn't feel it was spot-on, it was pretty good—a seven or eight on a ten point scale. Because I had struggled with infertility, *nurturing* sounded a little too motherly—at least to me—for someone who wasn't (and isn't) a mother.

My husband, on the other hand, was able to work through several word choices with Kevin for his 2-word purpose statement. He found that his statement just "clicked," and there was a great sense of it fitting. I was jealous that I didn't get that initial sensation.

I had battled depression for over twenty years. As I continued to focus on dealing with my depression, I went through a remarkable twelve-step program called Celebrate Recovery. Through that program, I was able to dig through a lot of the darkness and ugliness that was always with me. I was able to finally see myself as a beautiful person.

With this new growth and awareness, I revisited my 2-word purpose statement and determined the better fit for me of Discovering Beauty. Today, I can see daily how it plays out in my work and home life.

As a proofreader and copy editor, I like to be sure that everything is "perfect"—at least as much as it can be coming from an imperfect human. I find the beauty by pulling out the imperfections in the text so that the message can shine.

At home, I love it when I can take the time to declutter and organize—seeing the floor and cleared-off sections of my desk brings a sense of peace, calmness, and beauty, and even a bit of excitement. When working in these areas, there really is beauty and more joy.

I know it is helpful to revisit the process on an annual basis, but it has been a few years since I have really opened up my spirit to determine my wants. I know the tools are there, so I can go back and refocus myself.

The On-Purpose Person Process is something similar to the twelve-step program. It's in the day-to-day living where previous learning needs to be drawn upon. It helps to stay proactive rather than reactive to continue to take the time to Discover Beauty in myself and the world around me.

Purpose Facet

When you identify your 2-word purpose statement, your reaction will typically be one of the following three reactions:

1. "It's PERFECT!"—cue the heavens parting and the angels singing and you are certain that this is the moment you have waited for your entire life.

2. "It's OKAY"—not sure that it is right but interesting enough to walk it out for a while to consider it further.

3. "It's not there yet"—it doesn't feel right at all; it may be close, but needs more work.

All three reactions are fine and allow God to continue to reveal your purpose. It is hard work but so worth the effort!

When have you struggled with an issue, but with perseverance, you were able to arrive at a resolution?

ON-PURPOSE REFLECTIONS

_____

_____

_____

Karen

exists to serve by **Encouraging Faith**

En·cour·ag·ing: To give somebody hope, confidence, or courage; to motivate somebody to take a course of action or continue doing something; to assist something to occur or increase. Give confidence, cheer, support, persuade, push, promote, advance.

Faith: Belief in, devotion to, or trust in someone or something, especially without logical proof; a strongly held set of beliefs or principles, allegiance or loyalty to somebody or something. Confidence, trust, reliance, assurance, belief, devotion, loyalty, commitment, dedication.

Introducing Karen

So the first line of Karen's story is: My tendency had been to live life overcommitted and tightly scheduled. I am encouraged by her true life and transparency to help all of us along our similar journeys. I believe that Satan would love to isolate us and tell us "You are the only one that feels that way—everyone else has it all together." May your faith be encouraged by her story.

My tendency had been to live life overcommitted and tightly scheduled. My life definitely was not filled with purpose and peace. When I first read *The On-Purpose Person: Making Your Life Make Sense*, I was enthralled with the parable and wanted to engage in the described process.

I spent significant time away from my normal surroundings, making my Want Lists and pondering the process by myself. I eventually realized I needed someone to journey with me to provide encouragement and accountability. I began to focus and make headway toward living a purpose-filled life when a friend and I enrolled in the online On-Purpose Leadership Experience. We continue to be on-purpose accountability partners!

Identifying my "most important" want confirmed that I am designed to continually be learning and growing. Using the reverse tournaments, I gained tools to create a path with specific steps to learn and grow. I also have found that sometimes when I rework my want lists, I use another category to explore a specific short-term priority. For instance, I really needed to reduce clutter in my home, something I procrastinate doing. The Tournament process helped me to methodically accomplish this dreaded task.

My purpose statement is to the glory of God, I exist to serve by Encouraging Faith.

Encouragement is one of my gifts, and it can be multi-faceted. I instinctively search for possibilities, even in negative circumstances. Encouraging Faith is applicable in multiple life situations with people of all ages. I engage my purpose while mentoring fifth-graders as they learn new math skills. I also encourage family and friends to find a way through challenging circumstances. I can encourage faith in Jesus Christ, while leading a small group study with youth or adults.

I have become passionate about facilitating On-Purpose Peace for people to discern a personal, God-given purpose. It can be an arduous journey for people to recognize that God has been at work in their lives all along. I have observed amazing insight and transformation in the lives of people, as they realize that purpose is integrated into all of life. They connect the dots between the past, the present, and into a future of peace.

I have found that my vision statement has evolved over time, as my season in life changes. I've realized that I need to use my strengths to engage in fresh opportunities to grow personally, as well as to encourage, love, and inspire other people.

There are often challenges to staying on-purpose, because other people and life situations can cause unexpected opportunities or distractions. Personally, I need to find purpose in all that I do, or it isn't worth investing my time. Having my purpose in mind helps me filter options that come my way. Now I can more easily decline those that aren't a good fit, without a sense of guilt, and enthusiastically invest myself into those that I'm passionate about that are on-purpose for me.

Purpose Facet

Whereas Purpose is permanent, your Vision, Mission, Values, and what's most important right now in the life categories are opportunities for you to take reflective time perhaps on an annual basis, to recalibrate once again to stay on-purpose in all the aspects of your life.

This internal type of work is not "one and done." It is important to regularly reflect and refresh to provide ongoing insight and clarity as you move forward. Your long-term vision is one of those examples that is helpful to state and then revisit. Today, my vision for the next ten years is very different from the first time I did a ten-year vision back in 2001.

Think about your vision ten years from today. What would you like to be doing?

ON-PURPOSE REFLECTIONS

_____

_____

_____

Sarah

exists to serve by **Seeking Intimacy**

Seek-ing: Search for something, strive for something, ask for something, attempt something. Request, hunt for, look for, obtain.

In-ti-ma-cy: A close personal relationship, a quiet atmosphere, a detailed knowledge. Familiarity, closeness, understanding, relationship, confidence.

Introducing Sarah

Introducing my daughter's story is the icing on the cake for me so please excuse me if I gush. I remember our coaching time during a mother-daughter beach weekend and feeling excited and overwhelmed at the opportunity to help define my daughter's purpose statement. In coaching, there's typically a level of objectivity involved which is clearly much more difficult when you were there for her first breath. I could not be more proud of the woman and mother she has become as we grow to be an on-purpose family!

Another joy of including my daughter Sarah's story is that it emphasizes the importance of the On-Purpose Person Process and message, not only for us and this generation, but for the generations to come. Through it, we can ask ourselves: What is our legacy? How will they remember us? Did we live lives of purpose and joy?

The On-Purpose Person Process came to me at a time that I would guess is one of the most uncertain times in a person's life—the middle of college. I was uncertain of the future and even the present! I didn't really know what my goals were or what I was working toward, so any type of clarity or direction was needed and welcomed! I think I needed simple goals to focus on, since most of the big picture was up in the air ... and the Life Tournaments and 2-word purpose statement gave me clarity and some concrete ideas to go forward with.

As full disclosure, my mother is the author of this book and the one who led me through the process, so she had a small role in my choice to do this. I saw the impact of the process not only in her life, but also in the others she was leading through the process; so it was pretty good motivation to go ahead and try it myself!

When I look back on my Life Tournaments, my 2-word purpose statement, and my "most important want" ten years after the process, it's neat to see that many of the core wants I have are still the same. I am now married and have two daughters, with a third baby on the way, so of course my priorities and circumstances are different, but it's encouraging to know that this process helped me become aware of things that are true about me, regardless of how life changes.

The most significant part of the process for me was the 2-word purpose statement. No matter whether I was in college, on a cross-country road trip, experiencing my first years of marriage, or living in a town of 450 people with my husband and daughters—this statement has never stopped ringing true to who I am and what my purpose is. My statement is Seeking Intimacy, and I have found over the past ten years when I have made deep relationships and personal connections with God and others in my life a priority, I have without a doubt been on-purpose.

In contrast, there have been off-purpose times when I have felt stuck, isolated, and depressed—looking to myself or others for false intimacy (and for me that means relationships not grounded in the Lord). When I have not looked to the true source of love for my value and worth, I have felt very off-purpose and unfocused. So, I try to make sure that whether I am spending time coloring with my daughter, out to lunch with a friend, or choosing what to (or not to) watch on TV—that these activities are allowing me to add to a deep, meaningful, and authentic relationship with the Lord and those around me.

Purpose Facet

Beyond finding my own purpose, one of my greatest joys has been walking alongside my children as they discover and live into their own purpose. As a mother, there is deep heart longing for our children to discover God's purpose for their lives and I am grateful that both my children (and their spouses) have allowed me to share this process with them and are walking in His beautiful design for each of their lives. I am one happy On-Purpose Momma!

What would you like your legacy to be for the next generation?

On-Purpose Reflections

_____

_____

_____

I pray that you have been blessed with these stories of fascinating women from all walks of life who, just like each of us, are trying to know, discern, and live out God's unique purpose in each of our lives—during every season.

On-Purpose Stories

Giving

After years of working with women seeking to discover and live out their purpose, I have found that every single woman I have met truly wants her life to make a difference. Our purpose statements begin with: I exist to serve by ... so serving and giving are natural outgrowths of being on-purpose.

Pam Pugh with Women Doing Well always beautifully reminds us that we are made in the image of God and the familiar John 3:16 verse says in part, "For God so loved, he gave ... "—so we, like our heavenly Dad, are created to give.

Yet, as we give, many of us end up feeling overwhelmed, overworked, overspent, overused, and underappreciated. Each of these are classic symptoms of giving in ways God never intended for us and therefore off-purpose.

Here are some facts from the original research done by Women Doing Well—that may or may not be surprising to you:

- Christian women are 300% more generous with their financial wealth than the average American.

- Christian women are 400% more generous with their time than the average American.

Also from that research:
- Most women—4 out of 5—said they have capacity to give more.

- Only 6% of the 7,300 women who responded felt like they were a "Woman Giving Well"—one who lives with a strong sense of purpose and confidence, generously investing her time, talent, and treasure.

- The remaining 94% of the 7,300 desired to give more but needed to more clearly understand their purpose, identify their passion, and have a plan.

In our generosity and giving, purpose, passion and plan are defined as:

Purpose: As we now know, purpose answers "Who am I uniquely in Christ?" and "Why do I exist?"

With our giving, knowing our purpose allows us to say no to giving opportunities that are off-purpose and yes to those things that are more on-purpose for us. There is freedom when we do not need to say yes to everything but only to the things God has uniquely created us to do.

Passion: What do I believe in so strongly that I am willing to sacrifice for it?

Our passions should also guide our giving. These are the personal life experiences that have created deep connections for us with people groups or causes. In my own life, one of my passions comes from the traumas of my parents' failed marriages so our giving plans include ministries that focus on strong healthy marriages. Our passions can change throughout life but the needs of the world that most hurt our hearts will guide our discernment for our passions in giving.

The place God calls you to is the place where your deep gladness and the world's deep hunger meet.
— Frederick Buechner

Plan: What would God have me do with all He has entrusted to me?

A giving plan is needed as we consider what God has entrusted to us—not only in our financial resources, but with our influence, intellectual and personal resources—our time, talent, and treasure. The process to develop our giving plan includes thinking about how much we will share, save, and spend—and our vision of where we would like to be in our giving plan.

Steward your giving.
Learn to say "no" to off-purpose situations and
be free of guilt or "should's."
If you say "yes" to every request, you risk becoming
empty, angry, and resentful.
Off-purpose giving is stressful and leads to burnout.
Focus on on-purpose giving opportunities.

— From *On-Purpose Peace*

If your giving is currently feeling a bit dry and off-purpose, it may be time to reassess and decide whether you need to

- **Have the freedom to say no.**
  In my own life, I often hear about a need and immediately jump in to solve it because "somebody has to
  do it." Many times, I then find myself in off-purpose territory feeling tired, drained, and regretting
  my decision. The Lord then gently tells me that He
  actually had someone else in mind for that task, but
  because I was too quick to jump, they couldn't step
  into the need. The Bible shows us that even Jesus did
  not do everything that people asked of Him. Jesus
  was clear on His purpose, and we need to have the
  discipline and freedom to do the same.

- **Turn off-purpose giving to on-purpose giving.**
  Sometimes we can think about our giving that may
  feel off-purpose and turn it to on-purpose giving.
  My favorite story comes from an Inspiring Generous Joy experience, when a woman shared that she
  felt very off-purpose when she would go through her
  closet quarterly and leave bags of clothing on her
  front porch to be picked up by a local agency. When
  she shared that her purpose statement was Nurturing
  Worth, I asked if she would feel more on-purpose if,
  instead of leaving the clothes on the porch, she would
  actually go to the women's shelter herself and deliver
  the clothes and get to know the women there and
  "nurture their worth." Her eyes grew big and sparkled
  as she said, "That would feel so much more satisfying
  for me!"

- **Discern when God is asking us to give in obedience
  and give anyway.**
  There are times when God leads me to give even if
  I do not see it as perfectly on-purpose for me. God
  may specifically call me to write the check, organize a
  luncheon, attend an event, or quietly sit with someone
  at the hospital. I smile when I imagine that many

of the saints in the Bible may have initially felt that what God was asking them to do was off-purpose for them (think Moses, David, Joseph, Esther, Ruth, Mary, Paul …). Sometimes out of obedience, we are simply to say "Yes, Lord."

So let each one give as he purposes in his heart, not grudgingly or of necessity; for God loves a cheerful giver. — **2 Corinthians 9:7 NKJV**

Quite a thoughtful verse to ponder: in our giving of our time, talent, and treasure—are we typically cheerful givers or do we give reluctantly or give under compulsion? I believe the answers are yes, yes, and yes.

- Yes, at times, we are cheerful givers—full of joy, fulfillment, satisfaction, and the deep sense of God's pleasure as we generously give of ourselves.

- Yes, at times, we are reluctant givers—Webster defines reluctant as *unwilling and hesitant; disinclined.* Any giving that comes to mind when you have been a reluctant giver?

- Yes, at times, we give under compulsion—Webster defines compulsion as *the action or state of forcing or being forced to do something; constraint.* Any giving that comes to mind when you have given under compulsion?

Perhaps an interesting reflective exercise would be to consider what percentages of your giving *today* would fall under each category above?

So how can we be *more* cheerful in our giving *more* of the time? I have found that when we are giving out of our God-created uniquely designed purpose, we ARE more joyful.

I encourage you to think about all your current giving opportunities—ways you are and could be giving with your time, talent, and treasure. With your purpose statement in mind, ask the question—is this opportunity on-purpose for me? Or, is this request off-purpose and perhaps I should say no to this opportunity so that I can say yes to others that are more on-purpose for me? Remember, something that is off-purpose for you may be perfectly on-purpose for someone else—so perhaps you were not supposed to do it in the first place!

Or if there is a long list of opportunities that look good to you, one helpful way to prioritize our giving options is to create a want list of the ways you might be considering giving of your time, talent, or treasure. And as we have done before, run a Tournament—this time consider each pairing through the filter of your purpose statement to determine which of the two choices is MORE on-purpose for you. The winner of the tournament will show which giving opportunity is most on-purpose for you.

So many of the women who have attended the Inspiring Generous Joy conferences have begun to see how their giving can be more joyful and on-purpose. Here are several giving stories of women who are using their purpose to help guide their giving.

Sharon

exists to serve by **Cultivating Understanding**

Cul-ti-vat-ing: To improve or develop something, usually by study or education; to break up soil with a tool or machine, especially before sowing or planting. Develop, nurture, promote, encourage, work on, foster support, help.

Un-der-stand-ing: Ability to grasp meaning, knowledge of something, mutual comprehension. Thoughtful, considerate, comprehension, insight, awareness, appreciation, sympathy.

Reintroducing Sharon

You may remember my friend Sharon, introduced previously in On-Purpose Stories at Work. She is one of the founders of Women Doing Well and is passionate about generosity and giving on-purpose. Isn't it nice to know that even someone like Sharon is walking alongside of us—not miles ahead—when it comes to how we can all come to deeper understanding of our generosity and purpose?

My 2-word purpose statement of Cultivating Understanding coupled with my passion for young leaders helped target the giving of my time and financial resources this year. It also helped me say "yes" with confidence and "no" to off-purpose opportunities presented to me.

One example would be the opportunity I received to serve on the Board of Trustees for a major Christian University. As I prayed about my response, I realized that it was squarely on-purpose and in my area of passion. It was one of the highest and best uses of my generosity of time and skills. After this first year, I can confidently say that I am making a difference by cultivating understanding and am experiencing great joy in this on-purpose giving.

Another example is our year-end financial giving. In previous years, I've wrestled with how to respond to the emotional appeals we received for funding clean water and housing needs. I've experienced guilt for not making those appeals a major part of our giving portfolio. This year, I realized that God had raised up others with a purpose and passion for those human service ministries, and it was with joy that I was able to instead target funds for leadership development to cultivate understanding.

Purpose Facet

Have you ever considered your giving of time, talent, and treasure—and what is most on-purpose for you (life-giving, joyful, effortless) and what is most off-purpose (draining, dreading, and joyless)? Have you considered that perhaps what is off-purpose for you might be on-purpose for someone else?

What current giving is most off-purpose for you?

ON-PURPOSE REFLECTIONS

_____

_____

_____

Tami

exists to serve by **Building Confidence**

Build-ing: To form or develop something such as an enterprise or a relationship, or be formed or developed. Increase, create, encourage, foster, form, assemble.

Con-fi-dence: Self-assurance or a belief in your ability to succeed; belief or trust in somebody or something, or in the ability of somebody or something to act in a proper, trustworthy, or reliable manner; a relationship based on trust and intimacy. Self-assurance, poise, trust, support, loyalty, conviction, certainty.

Reintroducing Tami

Another follow-up story is from Tami in the On-Purpose Stories at Home section. I'm amazed at how each of our life stories and experiences always bring us into fresh new perspectives about our giving. God is so good about planting messages in advance of when we will need to put them into practice. It is certainly an ongoing adventure!

During the last few years, I've been involved with Women Doing Well encouraging women to live more joyful, generous lives so I've been very intentional about making joyful and purposeful giving decisions.

About a year ago, my sister went to be with Jesus. One of our first family discussions was to answer the question "How might we honor her" and allow others to do the same? It didn't take us long to decide to endow a scholarship in her name!

This endowment will provide an annual scholarship for a college student to study special education. It honors my sister's lifelong career as a special education teacher where she taught special needs students for many years. Even after she became disabled, she continued to teach ESL and learned sign language to work with students who had developmental challenges.

This was a very large gift for us—and one we had absolutely no question about granting. I can see that this gift truly aligns my purpose—Building Confidence—with my passion for education. It was truly a joyful decision!

Purpose Facet

Oh that we might all have such joyful decisions in our giving! To give with a joyful heart must really please God and I know brings such life to our souls. Think about the most joyful time in giving (time, talent, or treasure) that you have ever had—you knew God had called you to this opportunity and you could give joyfully and without hesitation.

What has been your most joyful giving experience?

On-Purpose Reflections

_____

_____

_____

Julie

exists to serve by **Cultivating Change**

Cul-ti-vat-ing: To prepare; to loosen or break up the soil; to foster the growth of; to improve or develop by careful attention; foster; nourish; promote.

Change: to make different; to give a different course or direction to; to undergo a modification; to pass from one phase to another; remaking, revision; transformation.

Introducing Julie

Julie is one special lady in my life and I am also very grateful to have had the privilege and blessing to coach her husband through the On-Purpose Person Process. Boy, when you get a couple both individually and together turned on about giving and On-Purpose—watch out world!

Like most couples, my husband and I are very different. When it comes to engaging with others, I love being part of high impact projects and events and he loves going deep with details and people. We married later in life so we came to marriage with a good sense of who we were and we both had giving practices and beliefs that were well established.

It all started to change two years ago when my husband lost

his job. He had just made a risky move to leave a stable corporate job to work with a smaller start-up firm. Having watched him struggle in his career to find satisfaction, I was sure this was the opportunity he needed. But God had other plans.

I remember the day he came home, just four months after starting the new job, to say he had been let go. Fear and uncertainty gripped my heart and I struggled to see how this could be good. I happened to be working with Mary on a project when Gary lost his job and she offered to take him through the process in an accelerated way.

For both of us, knowing our unique purposes has helped us navigate this very challenging two-year season. It has also helped us understand how we can both enjoy living and giving on-purpose even with our differences. My 2-word purpose is Cultivating Change while Gary's is Assuring Significance.

We both love to be involved and give our LIFE (labor, influence, finances, and expertise) to things we feel passionate about. I especially like to be involved in projects and giving my time.

During the same season Gary lost his job, I was feeling disconnected from our church community. Truthfully, I had never felt great about it, but I thought I should just be content where God had us. In the four years we had been members, I had been invited to help with many of what I would call "steady state" initiatives. I longed to engage, but our large church seemed to only need people willing to fill a spot—not cultivate change as I would enjoy.

When an opportunity came up to start a new community engagement effort, we quickly realized this would both satisfy my need to cultivate change by starting something new and Gary's desire to assure significance since the purpose of the project was to more meaningfully connect people in our congregation and help them go deeper.

We have also found knowing our purpose statements helps refine our financial giving. Coming into the marriage, we both had many things we supported with our giving. Because of the unemployment, we were forced to cut back our giving, and this has allowed us to refocus our giving to things we both get excited about. Giving is now something we do more intentionally together. Our purposes are not the only thing we consider when presented with an opportunity to give, but we definitely use them as a tool to discern what might be best.

As a wife, I long to both live and give on-purpose with my family and to those God has put in my path. Knowing my unique purpose and understanding my husband's unique purpose through this difficult season has brought a level of joy and satisfaction to our living and giving I didn't know was possible.

Purpose Facet

Many times at the Inspiring Generous Joy Conferences, the question is asked, "How can I include my spouse in what I have learned?" Sharing from your heart about what you are thinking is a start but it takes time. It's been almost four years since I started with Women Doing Well and the Lord has finally given me an opportunity to share this message with my husband at a Journey of Generosity (JOG).

What would you like your spouse or closest friends to know about your reflections and insights about a life of living and giving on-purpose?

ON-PURPOSE REFLECTIONS

_____

_____

_____

Della

exists to serve by **Inspiring Trust**

In-spir-ing: Having an animating or exalting effect; causing emotional stimulation; breathtaking; stirring; touching, enchanting; exciting.

Trust: Assured reliance on the character, ability, strength, or truth of someone or something; confidence; faith; certainty; hope; reliance, belief.

Introducing Della

Being around Della is like a big dose of God's joy and grace. Over dinner one night, she shared some of her story and I was so inspired that I asked her to share it with you. I love her transparency and honesty about our people-pleasing ways. But what inspires me most is that she is now sold out to God and His love shines all over her face.

Attending the On-Purpose Living and Giving workshop and learning that my 2-word purpose statement was Inspiring Trust was life changing. Not only did it impact the way I give, but it was another one of those gems that God puts in our lives to help us continue to transform our life.

It made me realize that my expressions of giving had been prideful and self-centered. The majority of my giving had been focused on family and friends. It made me happy to constantly buy "stuff" for them. I loved for people to think I was kind and thoughtful.

I did some giving out of guilt to my church or to the homeless shelter because I felt I was supposed to. Was my giving pointing to the grace of God and his generosity to us? Absolutely not! Was my giving really helping those with the most need? Absolutely not!

I discovered that Inspiring Trust has very deep roots for me personally. It's about my trusting God. It's about allowing God to inspire trust in me. Learning my unique purpose gave me tremendous clarity for my future giving journey. I want to give in a way that expresses God's love for his children.

"Do not store up for yourselves treasures on earth, where moth and rust consume and where thieves break in and steal; but store up for yourselves treasures in heaven, where neither moth nor rust consumes and where thieves do not break in and steal. For where your treasure is, there your heart will be also." — **Matthew 6:19–21**

My giving is no longer meaningless. I no longer desire to impress people. I no longer need to be acknowledged. I no longer need to buy people more stuff. My heart is geared toward eternity. I can't fix all the problems in the world but I can definitely make a difference to impact the life of another.

Giving has become a privilege because I want to please God. God owns it all. It is not mine to be stingy with. I am learning how to be a money manager of what God has blessed me with.

The more I trust God, the more the Holy Spirit propels me into the lives of other women including many whom I don't even know. I started worrying that some of them were going to think I was a stalker or that I was crazy. I mentioned this fear one day to a very special woman who has been a mentor to me and she said, "Remember, some people thought Jesus Christ was crazy. Do what the Holy Spirit leads you to do and don't worry about anything else." It turns out these women don't think I am crazy. As a matter of fact, many have told me just the opposite. My fear is gone and I step out in faith and trust God.

As a result of learning about on-purpose giving, I changed my giving habits. The percentage of my giving has increased significantly. I became so anxious to give that I noticed my charitable giving was all over the chart. I decided to conduct a personal "charitable giving audit." The result was that I was definitely giving off-purpose. I was giving to twenty different organizations. It wasn't aligning with my purpose or my passion.

I made a list of the causes that I care most about. I wanted to help people internationally as well as help people in my own community. It totally changed my giving pattern. Now I support my church, and charities and ministries that bring clean water to Ethiopia; that educate children in Africa; that support missionaries as they spread the gospel; that fight for children's welfare and safety; that teach people what God says about money and finances; that care for the homeless; and that deal with modern day slavery and sexual exploitation. My focus now is on Justice, Poverty, Growth, Evangelism, and Church.

Praise God, I am a Woman Living and Giving On-Purpose!

Purpose Facet

Della's story reminds me of the ultimate goal for a generous heart—no longer caring about what other people think or getting the admiration and credit but committed to giving more to the glory of God in the ways that He uniquely designed for us.

What is your vision for a life of living and giving on-purpose?

On-Purpose Reflections

_____

_____

_____

We are all on our personal giving journeys. Living and giving on-purpose provides clarity, freedom, and sense of knowing that we can give in the unique ways that God has created us.

Using your purpose statement as a filter enables you to make purposeful choices. In our world, there are many needs and giving opportunities. I believe God created us uniquely to fulfill only what He intended for us (not all of them all of the time) according to His designed purpose within us.

Could it be that God is resourcing women so that through their influence and through their giving, the world will experience a fresh wave of generosity to God's glory? —
Women Doing Well

Purpose Facet

As you consider the giving of your time, talent, and treasure—have you identified that which may be off-purpose for you, and that which is on-purpose for you?

On-Purpose Reflections

_____

_____

_____

Wholehearted
Purpose Resources

To help you continue your own self-discovery as a woman of Wholehearted Purpose, we've provided a wealth of resources at **WHPResources.com** where you can:

- Order and read *The On-Purpose Person*, the book that ignited my passion for this message.

- Gather a group to work through the *On-Purpose Peace Fellowship Edition* workbook—a self-facilitated Bible study format.

- Download the free *Personal Purpose Statement Development Tool* to select a working purpose statement for yourself. (You now know the Tournament process, and your reflections in this book will guide your choices.)

- Download a free Discovery Guide which includes Tournament forms for your life categories.

- Enroll to receive free regular "On-Purpose Minutes" from Kevin W. McCarthy.

And more resources:

- Contact me for individual On-Purpose coaching—*mary@marytomlinson.com*. This work is both my business and my ministry, so don't let any concern over cost hold you back. The process involves either hourly coaching to explore your purpose work from this book or The On-Purpose Person coaching process which involves one-hour calls over eight weeks, a workbook, and about forty-five minutes per week of "homework."

- Join us at an Inspiring Generous Joy Conference: *www.womendoingwell.com*.

- Explore *on-purpose.com*.

Whatever your next steps, my prayer for you is that you will follow that small quiet voice within you that whispers the wonderful truth that you have a unique design and purpose in this world, and you will bravely roll up your sleeves to begin the journey of a lifetime!

Closing Thoughts

"Being confident of this, that he who began a good work in you will carry it on to completion until the day of Christ Jesus." **—Philippians 1:6**

Always remember that our Creator had an amazing and perfect plan when He created YOU.

Psalm 139 has always been one of my favorites which speaks to the intimacy of our Creator and how He knows us deeply and has woven in our unique design.

"For you created my inmost being; you knit me together in my mother's womb. I praise you because I am fearfully and wonderfully made; your works are wonderful, I know that full well. My frame was not hidden from you when I was made in the secret place, when I was woven together in the depths of the earth.

"Your eyes saw my unformed body; all the days ordained for me were written in your book before one of them came to be.

"How precious to me are your thoughts, God! How vast is the sum of them! Were I to count them, they would outnumber the grains of sand—when I awake, I am still with you." **—Psalm 139:13–18 (NIV)**

My dear friend, it's time to discover and live your purpose; I promise you will never be the same.

About the Author

Mary Tomlinson is President of On-Purpose Partners, a firm specializing in personal/executive coaching, customer service, team and leadership development, branding, and the design and facilitation of planning retreats and workshops.

Sharing best practices, stories, and lessons learned from her career at Disney and in working with companies, organizations, and non-profits since 2001, she brings knowledge, insight, and a unique perspective to organizational challenges and opportunities.

On-Purpose Partners incorporates the transformational concepts from her business partner—Kevin W. McCarthy's books, *The On-Purpose Person*, *The On-Purpose Business Person* and *On-Purpose Peace*—integrating the keys to being on-purpose personally and professionally.

Prior to starting her own business in 2001, Mary spent 18 years at the Walt Disney Company in executive roles as:

- Travel Industry Director for Disney resorts world-wide with staff in Orlando, Anaheim, Tokyo, and Paris.
- Marketing Brand Director developing positioning strategies for Walt Disney World parks and resorts.
- Business Director of Walt Disney World's internal advertising agency managing 5,000 projects with a $130 million budget.
- Director of the former Disney Institute, a 585-room resort hotel and learning center with 800 employees, 100 training programs, and a $65 million budget.

Her first book was *Facilitation Made Easy: A Survivor's Guide to Great Meetings* and she has co-authored many published articles on teams and leadership.

She serves on the Advisory Board of Women Doing Well and as keynote speaker for their national "Igniting Generous Joy" conferences. She founded the Professional Christian Women's Group in Raleigh, where she and her husband moved in the spring of 2013 when her first granddaughter was born.

Mary is a high-energy business coach, speaker, and facilitator with a passion for encouraging individuals and implementing positive change.

www.marytomlinson.com

CPSIA information can be obtained
at www.ICGtesting.com
Printed in the USA
LVHW02s1526060518
576195LV00011B/568/P